GirlTalk

Hope, Humor and Hot Topics for the Young Heart

Sheri Rose Shepherd

SILOAM PRESS

GIRLTALK by Sheri Rose Shepherd
Published by Charisma House
A part of Strang Communications Company
600 Rinehart Road
Lake Mary, Florida 32746
www.charismahouse.com

Unless otherwise noted, all Scripture quotations are from the Holy Bible, New International Version. Copyright © 1973, 1978, 1984, International Bible Society. Used by permission.

Scripture quotations marked CEV are from the Contemporary English Version, copyright © 1995 by the American Bible Society. Used by permission.

Scripture quotations marked NLT are from the Holy Bible, New Living Translation, copyright ©1966. Used by permission of Tyndale House Publishers, Inc., Wheaton, IL 60189. All rights reserved.

Cover and interior design by Rachel Campbell

Library of Congress Catalog Card Number: 2001098702
International Standard Book Number: 0-88419-882-0

02 03 04 05   8 7 6 5 4 3 2 1
Printed in the United States of America

Acknowledgments

The list is endless of the people I want to thank for giving me the privilege of ministering and writing.

Barbara Dycus, you're amazing; thank you for catching my vision.

Dave Welday, thank you for making my dream to touch teen and college girls a reality.

Jamie Lynn, my faithful friend and inspiring writing coach... you gave me wings to fly.

Rochelle, you are the most comforting and calming friend I've ever had. Thank you for crying with me, praying me through the darkness and laughing at all my jokes.

Steven Gene, you're the husband who raises the standard of excellence in all men; thank you for never giving up on "us" and our family.

Jacob Andrew, my gift from God, I'm blessed to be your mom.

Emily Joy, you're the daughter I've waited my whole life for.

To all my "girlfriends" who helped me through this project... Susan, Rochelle, Chris, Jamie Lynn, Melinda, Judy, Monica, Danae and Nicole. Thank you for being "my eyes" to make the message in this book the best! I love you all for being my friends.

Frank and Marie at Conklin's Bed and Breakfast, thank you for opening your home for me to create and write.

Last, but not least, I thank God for turning my past mistakes into a ministry with a message of hope.

Introduction

Believe it or not, statistics say we girls use an average of thirty thousand words a day to express ourselves. If this is true, it's amazing that some of us don't hyperventilate and pass out between sentences! We do more than talk, though. We're actually multitalented. We can talk and listen to each other at the same time! How about the ladies' restroom? Now there's a "GirlTalk Conference Room." We have a buffet of subjects we talk about—everything from boys, beauty and bloating to dieting and depression, moms and money and, of course, shopping. If we're so good at communicating, why do so many of us still feel so alone in our struggles? Because we need more than thirty thousand words—we need real answers to real issues that affect all of us at some level in life!

I'm a former Mrs. United States, but my real title should be "*Mis*Understood." I mean, how many beauty queens talk about "Barbie Bondage?" And how many authors do you know who are dyslexic? (If you have trouble understanding me, just read this book backwards!)

I'm not the only one who holds the title of " *Mis*Understood." With so many mixed messages it's hard to figure out who we're supposed to be or what we're supposed to look like. It's time to clear up the confusion and have some fun. If you're ready to laugh and learn to be happy with you...then grab your favorite drink, snuggle up in a special place and let's get into some real GirlTalk.

YOUR FRIEND,
SHERI ROSE

Lord, if I can't be thin...
make all my friends
FAT!

Chapter One

Beauty Talk

Pop quiz time! Grab your number 2 pencil, close your textbooks and jump right in.

Barbie Bondage *quiz*

Are you in "Barbie Bondage"?

1. Whenever I go to a party, I need two hours to "primp." Anything less than that and my panic alarm goes off.

    ❑ True

    ❑ False

2. I have a love/hate relationship with my mirror. Some say we're very close. Whenever we're in a room together, we're constantly exchanging glances.

    ❑ True

    ❑ False

3. I have frequent appointments with a small box on the floor in my bathroom. It likes to make me feel like I'm not thin enough.

❑ True

❑ False

4. When I go out with my girlfriends, I secretly compare myself to them—my looks, my clothes, my hair, my weight… etc.

❑ True

❑ False

5. Shopping is more than an opportunity to buy stuff or to be with my friends. It's a mission to find that one outfit or accessory that will make me happy and attract attention.

❑ True

❑ False

6. When it comes to basic intake requirements, my body needs the following daily:

❑ One long stare from at least one boy (or three short stares from three different boys).

❑ Three compliments on my outfit or accessories (from a girl or boy).

❑ Two compliments on any other body part.

❑ One jealous look from another girl.

7. Beauty magazines are extremely important to me. They are my inspiration, my guide, my source of fashion wisdom, relational insights and all things cool.

        ❏ True

        ❏ False

8. I really don't like beauty magazines. They discourage me and make me feel very *un*beautiful. I can't help myself, however. I read them anyway whenever I get a chance.

        ❏ True

        ❏ False

9. If I'm totally "primped" to go out with my friends, and they don't rave about my outfit, I respond by pouting, crying, getting even, changing outfits or all of the above.

        ❏ True

        ❏ False

10. I have spoken or thought one or more of the following phrases in the last two weeks:

    ❏ She's so beautiful! I hate her guts!

    ❏ I would give anything to have her legs (her stomach, her eyes, etc.).

    ❏ I feel so fat!

    ❏ I'm not eating at all this week!

> **" When you discover what *real* beauty is, you will learn to *love* being you! "**

Please don't misunderstand me; I have nothing against Mattel's "Barbie" doll. As a matter of fact, I'm kind of envious of her. She's a little miss "hard-body" without weight-lifting; she wakes up with perfect makeup, no "bed-head." And she never says the wrong thing because, well, she can't talk. So how did she ever get so popular? Like me, millions of young girls—and young men— grow up learning about what is *beautiful* and what is *attractive* from this perfectly perky piece of plastic.

It's not Barbie's fault. I'm not saying we should banish Barbie. In fact, she is only a symbol of what we see all around us. Though Barbie doesn't talk, she has a message for all of us. It's the same message we see on television and in movies, music videos and magazines. Although it is whispered to each of us, the message comes in loud and clear: "You are not *pretty* enough, and you need to perfect your body and your image."

When we hear something often enough—no matter if it's true or not—we tend to believe it. I know I did (especially as a young girl). And when you feel something *deeply* and believe something *strongly*, it will affect the way you think and act. It can either *free* you or *bind* you up.

So, what is Barbie Bondage? It's that feeling you get when you look in the mirror and say:

"My body is not good enough."

"I'm not a valuable person because of the way I look."

"I can't succeed because I'm flawed."

"I need to dress this way in order to be loved and accepted."

We girls love to talk about beauty, and that's OK. But when you discover what *real* beauty is, you will learn to *love* being you!

Unfortunately, I had to learn the hard way that real beauty can't be bought in a department store or found in a fashion magazine. A low-cut dress or a navel ring may get attention, but they can't buy love. Plastic surgery may change our appearance, but it can't change a heart. Expensive makeup may cover up our blemishes, but it won't hide our insecurities. Don't misunderstand me; I think it's great to look your best, find your haircut, know what colors to wear and eat healthy and exercise. I'm all for making every effort to become the best version of you. One of my goals—my prayers—for our time spent together in this book is for you to be able to look in the mirror—not just at your face or your body—but at your heart and be truly thankful for who you are so you can be free to accomplish great things.

If anyone was ever destined to fall into Barbie Bondage, it was me. I was born to parents who both graduated from Hollywood High School. My dad became a popular disc jockey for a Los Angeles radio station and was always surrounded by beautiful women. He loved the whole Hollywood scene and hosted beauty pageants. My mom was an actress and singer; she even had her own television talk show in LA. For me growing up, life was a *show,* and I wanted to be the *star*! I dreamed about winning beauty crowns, modeling for magazines and people adoring the way I looked.

Have you ever had a Kodak moment? One of those frozen glimpses of time when everything all of a sudden became clear?

I was sixteen at the time. I begged my stepmom, Susie, to shoot me (with a camera, that is). There I sat, poised in front of the camera, proud as I could be because I had stuck to a healthy, low-fat diet for over twenty-four hours! Susie gently encouraged me to wait a few weeks to take the photo, but I pleaded, "I feel thin enough today to suck in, so hurry and take the photo before I pass out!"

Have you ever heard the saying *a picture is worth a thousand words*? I was excited to see this photo, but when Susie showed it to me, it left me speechless—which is almost impossible to do! I'll never forget the way I felt when I saw my *before* photo. *Is this really me?* I was shocked to see myself hiding behind all that extra weight.

To make matters worse, it was prom season, and all my friends had dates except me. I was so desperate to go that I actually paid my best friend's brother to take me. (I rented his tux, bought his corsage—everything!) At the prom, a popular boy grabbed my attention when he smiled at me from across the room and announced to the group, "Hey, Sheri, are you going to the beach party after the dance?"

"I'm not sure," I responded. "Why?"

His answer boomed from across the room, "Because you look like a beached whale!"

I was devastated by the hurtful words and the public humiliation. I ran to the bathroom sobbing. As I stared at myself in the mirror, my self-pity turned to anger, and my anger turned to action. I swore that day that no one would ever call me *fat* or *ugly* again! Through tear-filled eyes, I set my mind on a new journey—a quest for physical perfection!

The next day, my dad took me to the health club across the

street from my high school. Back then, they weighed you in, took your measurements and sat down and asked you about your personal goals. When the health club manager asked me my reason for joining the club, I announced, "I am going to be Miss USA! Can't you tell?"

He laughed with me and said, "Sure you are..."

For the next year, I worked out faithfully every day after school. My stepmom helped me eliminate white sugar, soda and fast food from my diet. (I think it's called "fast food" because it's better to *fast* than to *eat* it!) I even gave up partying with wild friends.

After one year, I had lost over fifty pounds. Then my mom took me to Nordstrom for a makeover. We must have spent over $400 on makeup and beauty treatments. It was so much fun! After I bought my new face, it was time for a new wardrobe! That's where my dad's credit card really took a hit. Prior to this shopping spree, I had never wanted to shop because I hated how I looked in my clothes. I only wore sweats, flip-flops and men's large shirts.

I was on my way to compete for my first beauty pageant. I was ready to give those judges a performance they would never forget. I thought I was totally prepared—modeling classes, speech training, catching up on current events. Part of every pageant is when the contestants do "the walk with the wave," parading one at a time down the runway toward the audience. The runway and stage were lined with tiny little lights, and spotlights followed each contestant like a movie star as they walked down the runway in their beautiful evening gowns. Keep in mind I had dreamed about this moment since the time I was a little girl. It was my turn. I walked excitedly down the runway toward the

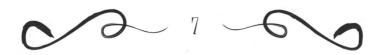

"It's not how we act; it's how we react that makes us a winner."

light beaming in my face. Yet I managed to smile and do "the wave." I took one step after another until there was nothing left to step on. I was literally walking on air for a brief moment and went flying through space off the end of the runway. I landed smack in the middle of the judges' table. The audience gasped.

Have you ever noticed that whenever you do something great no one is there to see it, but when you do something stupid it seems like the whole world is there to witness your "most embarrassing moment"? OK, back to my most embarrassing moment: As I eloquently rolled off the table onto the floor, the thought occurred to me, *I still want to win.* Mustering up the perkiest smile I could, I crawled back up on the stage, looked at the judges and said, "I just wanted you to remember me!" They did, and I won the pageant. We all fall down at some time in life (maybe not off a stage), and we all want to win—and we can. You see, it's not how we act; it's how we *react* that makes us a winner.

After my victory, all I could think about was food. I was so excited to go pig out on Mexican food that night wearing my crown and banner so all could see that "Sheri the Whale" was finally the "Fit Fish of the Sea." When I arrived at the Mexican restaurant, everybody was staring at me. Of course they were— I was wearing ten thousand rhinestones between my crown, banner and sparkling dress. I'm surprised everyone didn't put on a pair of sunglasses for fear they would be blinded by all the light reflected off my dress, crown and banner.

They took my order of nachos and bean dip and gladly served me; then the cute waiter asked for my autograph. I was so excited about my first autograph that when I tilted my head to sign the napkin, my crown fell in the bean dip! That didn't stop me from eating the dip. As a matter of fact, I was so hungry from dieting, and I scarfed the food so fast, that I'm not even sure if I used my teeth at all! I left with salsa all over the front of my white rhinestone dress and beans crusted in my crown. When we got home I forgot the crusty crown was on my head as I was getting out of the car. I smashed the crown and broke the top off. Then running in the house to call all my friends at 11:30 P.M. to tell them I won, I tripped again on my high heels and scrapped both my knees and ripped my nylons. Needless to say, I'm a klutz. When you've only worn flip-flops and tennis shoes all your life, it's hard to do an act on four-inch heels and a long, tight dress.

I could not wait to go to school the next day and see the boy who had humiliated me at my prom! "Mr. Popular" would have to jump in the ocean of regret for what he said to me. I took several hours to primp for school that morning. I spent one hour on my makeup and another hour changing in and out of at least ten different outfits.

You would think that winning a beauty title, losing fifty pounds and buying new clothes and $400 of makeup and skin care would make me feel self-confident. But somehow it didn't feel the way I dreamed it would. As a matter of fact, I began to live for the words of praise about my new look. It felt great when I was being envied and adored, but I could never seem to get enough (kind of like chocolate). I became obsessed with tanning

> **" External beauty, no matter how good, without internal beauty and a godly purpose for living is meaningless. "**

booths, working out twice a day, shopping daily for new outfits with Dad's credit card, more beauty pageants, modeling school and monthly photo shoots so I could see myself in portfolios. I even got plastic surgery on my nose. A modeling agency signed me even though I was only 5 feet 6 inches tall. At the peak of my quest for perfection, I won the "Best in Swimsuit Award" at Miss USA. This should have been enough to feel beautiful, but I was a slave to Barbie Bondage.

One more beauty secret could not free me, nor could makeup and a whole new wardrobe dress up my empty soul. I was out of control, even though it appeared as if I had it all.

Reality hit again...I was more insecure than when I was overweight in T-shirts and flip-flops with no makeup or a beauty title.

I joined the eight million girls in America who battle with an eating disorder. Once again I was eating bad food. I could not handle the thought of being fat again, so I threw up every meal and exercised excessively. Six months into this self-destructive lifestyle, my kidneys were hurting, my eyes were always puffy and my head always hurt from throwing up. I was crying myself to sleep every night, and then I put on a "happy face" for my audience—my family and friends. I was so ashamed of who I really was and how I felt. I could not bear the thought to tell anyone the truth. I was out of control and losing it!

I can confidently tell you that external beauty, no matter how good, without internal beauty and a godly purpose for living is meaningless. Even the most loved princess of all time, Princess Diana, never saw herself as good enough; she also battled with an eating disorder.

Today most of our favorite TV shows, fun fashion magazines and hit songs bombard us with this message: "Unless you're a sexy babe with a perfect body, you're nothing!" Beautiful models, actresses and recording artists are sending this message, yet deep down inside, they share the same desire to be relieved from the pressure of physical perfectionism. Most of them would trade their good looks, fame and money for peace of mind and a meaningful relationship.

Whose Image Are You Imitating?

How do feel about yourself after looking through a magazine filled with models? Have you ever noticed that these models seem to be taller or shorter than we are, and their hair is always something that yours is not? They are never what we are and always seem beyond our reach. Who are these models we are longing to look like? Their names don't really matter because they're images of airbrushed perfection. What we see is not reality.

If you think about it, every day we are bombarded with images of what we're supposed to look like. One month thin is in; the next month round and curvy is the look. What about hair? Short, long, curly, bald... We see it, we want it! It's hard to define who we really are and what we're supposed to look like with so many mixed fashion signals flashing in our face. Even the models are

mixed up and insecure. I have never met a model or pageant winner who has ever been completely happy with her appearance.

How is it possible that someone we've never even met influences us so powerfully? While perfecting our looks, we have lost sight of who we really are—awesome girls created in God's own image for a divine purpose. Let this truth from the Master Makeover Expert (God) speak some truth to us:

> *Those people who make idols are nothing themselves,*
> *and the idols they treasure are just as worthless.*
> *Worshipers of idols are blind, stupid, and foolish.*
> **—ISAIAH 44:9, CEV**

It's time to change our idols to the things that really matter. Fame only lasts for a while, and beauty eventually fades with aging. No one will ever like you more because of how you look. If anything, they will like you less because they will feel jealous or envious. When I first lost all of my weight in high school, I thought my girlfriends would be happy and proud of me because I was finally thin like they were. However, I was shocked when they treated me like competition rather than their friend. Maybe they changed because I changed. When I wasn't obsessed with my appearance I was probably a better friend. It's difficult to balance the way you look with who you really are as a person. The true beauties try to bless people with who they are, NOT try to impress them with how they look!

I had to learn to let go of what I could not do in order to succeed in what I wanted to do. For example, I spent years wishing I had big hair. So one day I saw an infomercial on clip-in hair. I was so excited I bought two pounds of long blond hair extensions. I could not wait for my next speaking engagement so I could flip my newfound hair around on the stage. While I was busy showing off the hair that wasn't even mine, I didn't realize several pieces came unclipped when a lady hugged me before I stepped on stage. So there I was with hairpieces falling out all over the place. I learned that the hair God gave me is good enough, so now I've learned to style all four pieces of hair very well. With all kidding aside, I've learned to be content with who I am, not just physically but in all areas of my life. We all are unique. We can learn from each other, but do things in our own unique style. Beauty is being yourself and learning to like who you are and letting go of what you're not.

IRRESISTIBLE BEAUTY {S E C R E T S}

If you are ready to become irresistible, then let me share with you the five most effective beauty secrets I've ever discovered.

Beauty Secret #1—For beautiful lips, speak words of encouragement.

Have you ever used your words to hurt someone you care about, either by gossiping or by not using your brain to think about what's coming out of your mouth? Many times we don't realize how our words affect the way others feel about us. God's Word tells us that the power of life and death is in our tongue (Prov. 18:21). The things we carelessly say can ruin the entire course of our future (Prov. 21:23).

Think about the effect our words have on us—and others. It's always the last hurtful word that ends a friendship or sends our parents to a divorce court.

But we can also use our words to help rather than hurt, to

build up another rather than tear a person down. Our words can encourage rather than discourage and show love rather than hate. How exciting it is to know we can use those thirty thousand plus words daily to make a difference in a lot of lives.

My husband, Steve, who was a professional model with the Ford Agency, and I used to help find models and actors in Hollywood for movies, soap operas, fashion magazines and modeling agents. We traveled the country auditioning thousands and thousands of models, actors and singers each year. Once we selected a group of a hundred or so talented people, we spent a week with them in acting and modeling workshops, photo sessions and other preparation. When the week was over, top casting directors and agents would pick winners to go to Hollywood. We loved our job because we were able to help people live out their dreams. But as exciting as it was to watch these actors and models get discovered, it was more exciting to see their lives changed by sharing with them God's power and purpose for their future!

In one talent search in Seattle, Washington, we auditioned three thousand plus people. During the audition, a group of gang members showed up to cause trouble. To be perfectly honest, I was scared, and I started praying for God to protect everyone. As I prayed, a very strange feeling impressed itself upon my heart. I felt that God wanted us to let these gang members hang out with Steve and me for the week.

At the moment, I was inside the hotel lobby door, safely protected by security. But I could not stop myself from walking outside to talk to the gang. As I walked toward that gang, I thought to myself, *I'm either hearing from God, or I'm going to meet Him tonight in heaven.*

When I stood in front of them, I used my lips to love them with these words: "God has a great plan for your life. Don't blow it. You have a future."

Two gang leaders yelled back to me, "How would you know that, Barbie?"

"I know it because it's true," I

> ❝ God has a great plan for your life. Don't blow it. ❞

told them. I invited them to audition for acting and, if selected, to spend the week with us. They accepted my invitation. Every day of that week I was determined to use my lips to speak words of life to them. I've learned that people need to be loved the most when they deserve it the least.

After we had spent five days with them at rehearsals, workshops and photo sessions, I was so excited because they decided to shower and stop showing up for the day stoned on drugs. By the seventh day they were greeting us with hugs. At each session we conducted, on the last day of the talent search I always shared with all the contestants how God had dramatically changed my life.

This time, after my talk the two gang members, who were brothers, came to Steve and me and asked us to pray with them about their past. They told us that when they were only seven and eight years old, their parents had driven to Seattle where they pushed the boys out of the car and then drove away. Over the years they had been placed in many different foster homes— most of them abusive. They were now eighteen and nineteen years old and didn't know what to do with their lives. But they wanted to change—and they DID!

" Line your beautiful lips with words of love. "

To those gang members, we had more beautiful lips than the most beautiful cover girl model because our lips spoke God's words of hope, love and direction.

❀ Girl POWER Prayer ❀

Dear God, please forgive me for the times I've used my words to gossip or hurt someone. Help me to speak words that encourage others, including my family members.

You Go, Girl!

You too can have the most beautiful lips. You don't have to lower your standards to gab and gossip like the other girls. You can line your beautiful lips with words of love, hope and encouragement. Become irresistible to anyone who hears you talk!

Beauty Secret #2—For beautiful eyes, look for the best in others.

When we use our beautiful eyes to look for the best, we help others see the best in themselves. As a senior in high school, I had entered my "change-everything-about-me mode." One change I had made was to begin jogging. Slowly I jogged every

day around the one-mile track at my high school. Please keep in mind as I share my "Prince Running Back Story" that I was not popular with the boys in high school and was still in my new-found "change everything" mode.

One day, like a wimp I was running slowly around that track when, from the back of the bleachers, I heard someone yell, "Pick up your knees and run faster!" I looked over to see a typical "Mr. Jock," a very handsome, dark-haired guy I knew was on the football team. He yelled again, but I did not realize that he was yelling at me—good-looking boys had never noticed me before. So I ignored him.

He was determined to be seen, so he ran down on the track beside me and said, "Didn't you hear me? Get your knees up and run faster!"

"Why should I?" I asked him.

"Because you need to run harder if you're going to be the next Miss USA," he shot back at me.

"What makes you think I want to be Miss USA?" I asked.

"Last year when you were weighing in at the health club, I was standing in line right behind you," he told me. "I heard you tell the manager your goals."

Now I was really embarrassed, so I answered, "I was only kidding! I could never be Miss USA."

"I've watched you get off drugs and lose all that weight," he told me. "I think you can do anything. I'm proud of you." I started to cry tears of joy because no one other than my dad and stepmom had ever been proud of me or believed in me. I found out that this running back's name was Mark, but I call him "Prince Running Back."

After he finished running with me, he offered to train me for

the pageant. "What pageant?" I asked.

"The one I'm entering you in next year," he replied. I thought I must be dreaming. Someone had seen the best in me even before I had become the best version of me.

Prince Running Back did train me. He was also super smart, and he taught me all about politics and the history of our country. But most importantly, he taught me to believe that I could do anything if I would change the way I looked at myself and the world around me.

It was fifteen years later when I did finally win the national beauty crown. It wasn't Miss USA; it was Mrs. United States. That night when the pageant was over and I went back to my hotel room with my crown and banner, I knew that this victory was not because of me but because a stepmom and Prince Running Back had looked for the best in me with their beautiful eyes. In other words, they saw a winner even if I never won a crown. Then God, in His own timing, gave me a crown to use for His glory, not my own.

❀ Girl POWER Prayer ❀

Dear God, give me eyes to see the best in myself, and in others.

YOU GO, GIRL!

What you look for is what you'll find. I heard the story of two young girls who moved to a new city from two different towns.

18

When they arrived at their new school, they were both curious about what the other kids were like in that school. The first girl asked the teacher about the other students, and the teacher asked her, "Well, what kind of kids went to your old school?"

> **" Believe the best, and you'll find the best! "**

The first girl said, "They were all rude, jealous and mean." The teacher then told her that she would probably find the kids at this new school to be like the kids at her old school.

Later, the second girl approached the teacher and asked the same question: "What are the kids like here at this school?"

"Well, what were the kids like at your old school?"

The girl said, "They were really nice, fun and friendly."

"Well," the teacher said, "I'm sure that's what kind of kids you'll see here."

Do you get the message? Beautiful eyes look for the best. Believe the best, and you'll find the best!

Beauty Secret #3—For beautiful hands, reach out to someone in need.

Have you ever experienced the joy of being the hero in someone's day? There is nothing greater than knowing you have made a difference in the life of another person. My teenage son, Jacob, and I recently took a trip to Portland to shop. We live in a small town without a mall, so this was an exciting trip. We could not wait to spend the money we saved on new clothes for ourselves.

I love to shop. I call the mall "My Mother Ship." I must say,

this day turned out to be the ultimate shopping experience for Jake and me.

We walked into the mall and saw a young girl with black, dyed hair, five earrings in each ear, dirty, sloppy clothes and black lip liner—you get the picture. Because she looked distressed, I walked up to her and asked her if she was OK.

"What do you care?" she replied. So I asked if I could pray for her. As we were visiting, her boyfriend approached us, and he was more desperate looking than she was. They poured out their hearts to us. They were eighteen years old, homeless and sleeping under a bridge in the middle of winter. They had just given their baby up for adoption.

"Well, it's time for both of you to go on a major shopping spree!" Jake boldly suggested. So we took them shopping. We had so much fun picking out coats and clothes for them at Nordstrom's Rack. Seeing their faces lit up with joy was better than buying anything for ourselves.

When we finished, we prayed with them and gave them the rest of our cash. Jake says that was the most awesome shopping experience ever! To that young homeless couple, our beautiful hands were more beautiful than the best set of acrylic nails.

❀ Girl POWER Prayer ❀

God, use my hands to reach out to help someone today, whether it be my mom, my friend or a neighbor.

You Go, Girl!

On a sheet of paper, write down some ways you can use your hands to reach out to someone today. Maybe your mother needs help around the house. Maybe your neighbor needs a break and a free babysitter. Or maybe a friend needs you to listen to her with your heart. There are endless opportunities to use your beautiful hands to reach out to someone. Go for it!

Beauty Secret #4—For beautiful legs, take a walk down the right road.

While touring the country as Mrs. United States, one day I was driving a rental car in Detroit, Michigan. The church at which I was going to speak had given me specific directions for getting from my hotel to the church. I wish I had followed the directions, but being the adventurous person I am, and since I was running late, I decided to ask some stranger for a shortcut. The stranger wrote out completely different directions from those I had been given.

I didn't have a good feeling about the stranger's directions, but I used them anyway. Unfortunately, those directions led me in the wrong direction. I ended up in a bad neighborhood filled with crack houses and gangs. There I was—"Barbie with a Bible in the ghetto." I knew I had listened to the wrong person, thus putting my life in danger.

In desperation I prayed to the only One I knew who could get me back on the right road—God. Shortly after that prayer, a police officer came up to the car and offered to escort me back to the road that would lead to where I needed to go.

Once God got me going in the right direction, I started to think about how many wrong roads I had traveled following friends' directions that had led me to the wrong parties, wrong choices and the wrong boys. Many of us are on the wrong road now because we don't know what a right road looks like or who can give us the right directions. We don't have to drive our own way on the wide road to self-destruction. Be careful whose directions you follow. Look at the life of your leader before you decide to follow.

If they don't represent the way you want to live or where you want to go in life, stop and make a U-turn in the right direction before you end up in trouble.

❀ Girl POWER Prayer ❀

Dear God, please give me Your directions to the right road, which leads to life. Help me to share those directions with others.

YOU GO, GIRL!

Use your beautiful legs to walk the right road and to help you live the right life. Look for someone who needs directions to the "right road." Walk with that person to the starting point—which is a U-turn toward a relationship with God and the Word.

Beauty Secret #5—For a beautiful wardrobe, dress the best!

When I lost fifty pounds as a senior in high school, I was so excited that I couldn't wait to wear miniskirts, tightly cropped tops and backless sundresses. I had worked hard on my body, so why shouldn't I show it off, right? Besides, all my friends dressed in sexy clothes, and I loved the way boys noticed me when I wore those kinds of clothes. I never once thought about how much my clothes revealed the type of person I was inside until one day when I overheard some boys talking about our homecoming queen, a girl named Sarah. Sarah was the only popular girl at our school who never showed her belly button, back or breasts. She dressed in tailored pants, pretty buttoned-up shirts and shorts that never exposed her buns.

"Sarah is so awesome," I heard one boy say. "She is just the kind of girl I want to marry someday!"

I couldn't resist asking this question, "Why would you marry someone like that? She is so conservative, and she dresses like a dork!"

To my surprise, the best-looking guy at school said, "She is a class act. She's the kind of girl you want to be the mother of your children. The other girls are only good for one thing."

"What's that?" I asked.

"Sex," he answered. "That's why they dress like prostitutes. That's all they want!" I was in shock.

You see, Sarah had good girlfriends and the respect and adoration of even the most popular boys at our school. I also noticed that the teachers treated her special. She dared to be different and keep her body covered even though she was in great physical shape. She wasn't hung up on how she dressed. Her clothes

"Are you a copycat or a class act?"

were cute, but never sexy.

I decided that I wanted the boys to look at me as a "class act" also. I wanted to be someone they would want to marry someday. So I went home and told my step-mom that she had been right about my clothes being too sexy. We went shopping for a new look—the right look for who I wanted to be.

I learned that it's more fun to be different. I liked being the leader in a new fashion trend, and, best of all, people began treating me with respect and importance.

How about you? What message does your wardrobe give about who you are? Do your friends tell you what to wear? Are you a copycat or a class act? Let your beautiful wardrobe express that you are "God's Awesome Girl."

🏵 Girl POWER Prayer 🏵

Dear God, help me dare to dress differently than the fashion fanatics dress!

YOU GO, GIRL!

Join the "Class Act Club." Go through your wardrobe today, and get rid of everything that lowers the standard of who you really are. Don't wait! Be the one in your group of friends who sets the trend for others to follow. You're awesome!

Beauty in Action

" It's more fun to be different! "

When you buy makeup at a store, they usually have testers for you to try before you buy. I want to challenge you to test the irre-sistible beauty tips in this chapter for yourself. There is nothing more irresistibly beautiful than a girl who leaves beauty marks on someone else's life. Go ahead—look your best. But then put real beauty to the test. The best free samples are those we give when we give free samples of God's love to other through our own lives.

When I lived in Arizona, I met a group of young, beautiful girls who wanted me to help them start a volunteer team that could get involved in community projects. These girls were more than beautiful—they were in the winner's circle because their hearts purposed to make a difference, and their minds made a plan of action.

First we decided on a name for our team. It was called the "Arizona USA team." We met with several charities like Feed the Children, Teen Challenge, Help the Homeless, Special Olympics, children's hospitals and others. Not all of them were receptive to our help—but some were.

We printed T-shirts with our team name. We hooked up a voicemail hotline so girls on the team could call in and find out what was going on in the community. Charities, churches and ministries could also reach us if they needed the help of our team. To get the word out better, we printed personalized busi-ness cards for each girl who joined the team. The cards read, "Arizona USA Team—Making a Difference." They had an 800 voicemail number and post office box number for people to use for mailing information to us.

Once a month we would hold a free seminar at a local school telling girls about the team. Then they would have the chance to interview with some of the team members. From that, we broke the team down into groups that could be used to touch people in different ways. We started individual teams for dance, drama, speech, organizing, calling and serving.

Once we defined our dream to help our community, people started taking us seriously, and the phones began to ring off the hook. Almost every weekend we were scheduled for some event—singing at a children's hospital or retirement home, helping to organize a fundraiser, working with the Special Olympics and visiting children's orphanages to play with the kids or lead them in special activities.

Our purpose to help exploded with power. We started with ten girls, and, in one year, we had more than one hundred fifty girls on the team. But even greater than giving to our community was being able to watch the girls discover they were leaving beauty marks on people's hearts by being willing to help others.

Write down something you want to do to make a difference. Consider these examples: Volunteer at a church by helping in the nursery; call your local charities or ministries in the phone book to ask how you can help; start a girl's group and go through a video series together on some hot topic; baby-sit for a single mom; listen to a friend; bring flowers to someone elderly and alone in a retirement home; create a website for troubled teens; head up a fundraiser for something or someone in need; bring or serve food at a homeless shelter. Whatever you do, make sure it's not just about you, and you'll win.

IRRESISTIBLE BEAUTY {S E C R E T S}

- ❀ *Use your beautiful lips to* speak words of encouragement.
- ❀ *Use your beautiful eyes to* see the best in others.
- ❀ *Use your beautiful hands to* reach out to someone in need.
- ❀ *Use your beautiful legs to* walk your friends down the right road.
- ❀ *Use your wardrobe to* express how special and classy you really are.

There is nothing more beautiful than a girl who loves God with all her heart. You be that girl!

GOD TALKS
Beauty

God Is...the Beauty Makeover Expert

I used to love doing professional makeup and hairstyling for models at their photo sessions. It was amazing to see the transformation. A beauty makeover affected the way they felt about themselves because they loved feeling beautiful. Yet as beautiful as they looked in their makeup, at some point they had to wash off all that temporary beauty and look at their reflection in the mirror without all the glamour.

When God does a beauty makeover, He lights up your eyes with love. He radiates your face with a smile that can't be captured on a camera, only in real life. The greatest thing about God's makeover is that His beauty through you is a reflection people will never forget. God's makeover is free for the asking, but priceless to His princesses.

> Dear God, make me up to be beautiful in all I do and say. Let my life leave eternal beauty marks every day.

He has made everything beautiful in its time. He has also set eternity in the hearts of men; yet they cannot fathom what God has done from beginning to end.

—ECCLESIASTES 3:11

What is YOUR role in the "Movie of Life"?

Chapter Two

Talent Talk

Everyone dreams of being discovered for something! Talented writers want to be published; talented singers want a recording contract; scientists want to win a Nobel Prize for one of their discoveries; models want to be cover girls; actors want to be on Broadway in New York or star in a Hollywood movie. What do you want to be discovered for? Have you ever wondered what part you should play in the movie of life? Believe it or not, the producer/director of the whole universe (God Himself) has created a very important role for you to play.

When I was in high school, I always thought everyone was better than I was. I did not do as well as my friends in school because I had a learning disorder called *dyslexia*. Dyslexia causes you to see things backward, so if you are having trouble understanding anything in this book, read it backwards!

I didn't have the talent to sing like my friends who were

in choir. It amazes me how many people assume pageant winners can sing. Once, when I was booked in Nashville to speak, the church where I was speaking actually advertised in the local newspaper that Mrs. United States was going to sing the national anthem for their Fourth of July service. Boy, were they surprised!

I tried dance class once, but I was too uncoordinated to keep up with the class. As a matter of fact, when I was on NBC's nationally live telecast of "Miss USA," the choreographer decided to sit me on the piano bench for the opening dance number because I couldn't keep up during rehearsals, which caused the other girls to keep tripping over me! I've never been artistic, either. My two-year-old colors better than I do.

When I graduated from high school, I had no idea what I was going to be when I grew up. While I was waiting to find out, I took a job as a waitress because I loved food, people and cash in my pockets. By the end of my first day, I had heard that the tips were great. But not for me—on that same day I accidentally dumped a spinach salad on a bald man's head. He looked so funny that I started laughing as I tried to pick the spinach leaves off his head. I was fired on the spot!

My next adventure was in beauty college. I thought, *I like beauty, hairstyling and makeup. I'm sure I could do this!* Someone should write a "Survivor TV Show" about my time at beauty college! I was brutal! When it was time for me to work on my first victim (I mean woman), I took her to the shampoo bowl to wash her hair. I turned the water on, grabbed the hose and nearly fell to the floor as I slipped in some water. I quickly pulled myself up but noticed that my supersoaker hose had completely blown off the woman's false eyelashes! She was soaking wet and furious. Again, I could not control my laughing attack! She looked hilarious! My teacher was so mad at my reaction that I was "voted off the island"...suspended forever. At least I hadn't been holding scissors!

" God has a part for you to play in His theater of life. "

There were only two things I did well—talk and make people laugh. But I did not realize that my obsession to talk to any poor soul within five feet of my reach could be considered a talent, nor did I ever think God could use my ability to help people laugh at life as a talent to heal hurting hearts. I just thought I was a gabby goofball.

Today I'm still amazed that I get paid to do what I love—travel, meet people and talk at conferences, churches and retreats. In the same way that God gave me a part in His theater of life, He has a part for you to play.

Take the following "Talent Search Quiz." It can help you to discover your role in the movie of life.

GirlTalk *quiz*

Talent Search...Discover the true you!

Check the answer that best describes you. Total your scores at the end of the quiz.

1. If I were involved in a big Hollywood movie, I would want to...

   A. Star in the movie with my favorite actor.

   B. Direct or produce the movie.

   C. Create or write the movie.

   D. Help with behind the scenes stuff and watch it being filmed.

2. When I have to give an oral report in front of my class or coworkers...

   A. I can't wait to *wing it* in front of the class.

   B. I take it seriously and prepare quickly.

   C. I take time to think about it, and I am very concerned about doing a perfect job.

   D. I don't like being in front of people, so I procrastinate until the end, then do it because I have to.

3. Most of the time I like doing things...

   A. The fun way.

   B. My way.

   C. The right way.

   D. The easy way.

4. I consider myself more...

   A. Playful.

   B. Powerful.

   C. Perfectionist.

   D. Peaceful.

5. I like my friends to (rank the answer by most important to least important)...

   A. Play with me.

   B. Listen to me.

   C. Learn with me.

   D. Relax with me.

6. I like to be...

   A. Spontaneous; do things on the spur of the moment without plans.

   B. Sure; direct how things should go each day.

   C. Scheduled; follow an exact plan without changes.

   D. Easygoing; flow with the plans.

7. I want life to be…

    A. Delightful, fun and exciting.

    B. Daring, risk-taking and adventurous.

    C. Detailed, scheduled and in order.

    D. Consistent, even and easy with no conflict.

8. I am more…

    A. Forgetful, because details are not fun.

    B. Straightforward and bold about what I think.

    C. Frustrated when things or life gets out of order.

    D. Fearful and deeply concerned about people and life.

9. I…

    A. Had a lot of fun taking this test.

    B. Took this quiz quickly so I could get to the next chapter.

    C. Want to know why I had to take this quiz.

    D. Took this test because you asked me to.

10. I…

    A. Love to entertain people and make them laugh.

    B. Love to take charge and direct activities.

    C. Love to organize things and learn new things.

    D. Love to volunteer and help people.

11. When I'm bummed out I'm more...

    A. Restless and anxious.

    B. Harsh and impatient.

    C. Negative and critical.

    D. Depressed and quiet.

12. I'm more of a...

    A. Looneytoon.

    B. Leader.

    C. Learner.

    D. Listener.

Scoring Your Answers

Write down the total points in each category below:

As "Go Playful"   ____

Bs "Go Powerful"   ____

Cs "Go Perfectionist" ____

Ds "Go Peaceful"   ____

If you scored mostly:

    As You're a "Terrific Terri Talker"

    Bs You're a "Diligent Debbie Doer"

    Cs You're a "Thoughtful Thelma Thinker"

    Ds You're a "Patient Pamela Peacemaker"

Let's Talk About Terrific Terri Talker

"You're great at living in the present."

OK, Miss "Life of the Party," who could ever have a party without inviting you? You're an amazing storyteller. You put color in our black-and-white world and laughter in our lives. You're like a precious puppy that needs to be trained, irresistible but sometimes irresponsible. You love your friends to listen to you and laugh at your jokes.

You're great at living in the present. You don't hold very many grudges, mostly because you can't remember them very well, so you don't dwell on past offenses. You can talk about anything at anytime with anyone without any knowledge of what you're talking about. You get depressed if there is nothing fun and exciting to look forward to.

Critical and negative people who don't respond positively to your cute personality hurt your feelings. You react to stress by exiting from the "not so fun situation"—by shopping, doing something creative or pigging out on your favorite food. If you had a choice, you would "dump the details" and get the good life of "fun in the sun" in the "wing-it world."

I'm a Terri Talker who doesn't pay much attention to details. When I was Mrs. United States, I was invited to speak at a very special Teen Challenge banquet. I was having a lot of fun talking and eating at the head banquet table, which was located on a stage. I did not even notice I was at the wrong banquet, sitting at the head table in someone else's seat, eating someone else's dinner. I should have been embarrassed when I discovered my error, but I just laughed, then quickly left and went to

Talent Talk

the place I was supposed to be.

I had a girlfriend who is a typical Terri Talker. One day she set out to go to the mall to buy some new hair care products. She asked her mom if she could borrow the car. Her mom said, "As long as you are back within two hours."

So with keys in hand and her "to buy list," which she lost before she got to the mall, she was off on an adventure. She entered the mall and ran into her friend Pamela Peacemaker. Pamela invited Terri to join her for lunch and a movie. Of course, Terri Talker could not pass on a good time with a girlfriend, so she said yes. She totally spaced out about the fact that her mom gave her a two-hour time limit.

After lunch and a movie, the girls went out to shop and discovered a great sale. After trying on twenty outfits apiece, each girl bought just one outfit. Then they went to the beauty counter to get a complete makeover. Terri was so excited about her makeover that she decided to slip back into the dressing room and put on one of her new outfits.

Oh no! she thought. *I need new shoes to match!* So she wandered back into the mall barefoot, on a mission to find matching shoes. While she was in the shoe store, she ran into another girlfriend who was on her way to dinner and a movie. Terri invited herself, and off she went for round two of a meal and movie. While she was in the middle of her second movie, it dawned on her that she was supposed to be home *eight hours earlier.*

She rushed out of the theater like a monkey climbing over people who were comfortable in their seats, than raced to the nearest pay phone to call her mom. While waiting in line she began searching for a quarter to make the call. While she was searching, she decided to go on an organizational binge and clean out her backpack purse.

Although Terri Talker knew she would probably be grounded for the rest of her life for being irresponsible, somehow she was still excited about all the things she was finding in the bottom of the backpack. She thought most of them were lost. Finally it was her turn to use the phone, but she had never found a quarter because she got distracted cleaning out her purse. So she smiled sweetly and borrowed change from a stranger in line.

She called her mom, who had called the police. She apologized to her mom and said, "I just lost track of the time!"

How is it possible that Terri Talker could forget her original reason for going to the mall (hair care), lose track of eight hours and still be happy about her day? Because Terri Talkers just want to have fun. When the Terri Talkers in our world are having a good time, they don't care what time it is and don't realize that the rest of the world is on a time schedule.

You Go, Girl!

It's time to give your gift away. Even though we love attention, the goal should not be to win people's approval, but to win their hearts. You're naturally gifted to work with people or in front of people. You would be an awesome public speaker, tour guide, interior designer, performer, hostess, hairdresser or sales rep for any company you believe in because you could probably convince Eskimos in Alaska to buy an ice machine for their backyard in the winter.

In other words, you're so convincing when you're communicating that people will buy whatever you're selling! However,

even though you have the gift of gab, take a break once in a while. You will be amazed what you can learn from listening to others.

Try not to be disappointed or discouraged by the people who don't share in your enthusiasm to "live life the fun way." You were born to color the world, but some of your friends and family have been gifted differently. They may be like Debbie Doer, gifted to conquer and keep control of the world. Or they may be Thelma Thinkers who have been gifted to correct and perfect the world. Maybe they are a Pamela Peacemaker and can comfort and calm the world.

> **"The purpose of opening your gift is to give it away."**

The purpose of opening your gift is to give it away. There is no reason to compete with or compare yourself to another person. There is a very important reason to get a part in God's movie of life—it's a "blockbuster," one you don't want to miss!

Pay attention to these details, and it will increase your ability to function in the real world. Don't use your gift of gab to gossip. Learn to keep track of time, meaning, use your watch for more than a fashion statement.

Just because you wing it well, remember that the rest of the world is on a schedule. Get a daily organizer system to keep track of lists, phone numbers and other important details. Make sure that it is a bright color so you aren't as likely to lose it. Put your name and phone number in it so people can return it to you when you do misplace it!

> 66 You're an adventurous risk-taker who loves to explore new territory! 99

Let's Talk About Diligent Debbie Doer

If you are Diligent Debbie Doer, you love living life on the edge. You're an adventurous risk-taker who loves to explore new territory! You like people who follow your lead and don't get in your way. You're a woman who knows what you want, and you won't settle for second best. You don't need fluff; you want facts. You were created to conquer. People will always know where they stand with you because you don't play games. You say what you mean and mean what you say. I love that about you!

I love Debbie Doers because Debbie is everything I am NOT. I had a great business manager who was a Debbie Doer. She was not afraid to take on any challenge; maybe that is why she accepted the job of managing me. She could do the work of three people but twice as fast. I was amazed to watch her performance. She remained in control when everyone else was losing it! She was the dynamic person who dared to dream the impossible. She was motivated by making magic happen while the rest of the world watched in amazement.

At age twenty she went on a missions trip to a Third World country. She saw the hopelessness of the people's situation to get food and shelter, so she found the persons responsible for helping to facilitate getting their living necessities. Then she observed their system. Before long, Debbie used the facilitator as a translator to tell the country's leader about a better way to meet the needs of the citizens. Only Debbie Doer would aggressively pursue a leadership position in a country where she couldn't even speak the language!

But it worked. She helped them to institute a better way before she left. That's why we need Debbie Doer—she excels in urgent situations.

Diligent Debbie Doers love to tell people what to do. My two-year-old, Emily Joy, is a Debbie Doer. She constantly tells me what to do and where to put things. One day we were doing some shopping in a Target store, when I put something back on a shelf where it did not belong. "Mommy, that does not go there! Put it back now!" she told me.

"Emily Joy, you are a bossy girl," I told her.

"You're a bossy mommy," she shot back at me. Even when she's in trouble for not obeying me and I have to remind her I'm the boss, she still reminds me that she is the boss of all her toys and dolls.

You Go, Girl!

As a Debbie Doer, you are happiest when you're leading a project or going after a goal. What people think of you is not your number one priority. That's what makes you a great leader.

You would make an awesome director for big events, a business owner, lawyer, doctor, politician, CEO of any company or a great public speaker who is able to motivate people to action. You could also be a great mother for a large family. Without your talent the world would not have strong, competent leaders, and God knows we need someone to give clear-cut directions.

> " *The goal is to bless, not to boss.* "

Remember that the goal is to *bless*, not to *boss*. To lead well, you must learn to love well. People don't care how much you know until they know how much you care. Caring will get you where you want to go faster than criticizing. God didn't give you the talent to lead without the ability to love. People need love the most when they seem to deserve it the least. Don't run over your friends and family while trying to drive them on the right road. Wait for them to settle into your car and buckle up before you rush them to your destination of the day.

Try to remember that not everyone sees things as black and white as you do. Just as you were created to conquer and lead, your other friends have unique callings of their own. Pamela Peacemaker was created to calm and comfort. Terri Talker plays the role of encourager and excitement producer. Thelma Thinker will take the time to perfect a better way.

One word of caution for you, Debbie Doers: Cut the word *stupid* out of your vocabulary along with the question, "Don't you get it?" Don't cause those you love to feel inferior to your superior leadership talent.

Let's Talk About Thoughtful Thelma Thinker

Your incredible standard of excellence exceeds all the rest. You're deep, considerate, creative and do almost everything you do the right way—and do it creatively. You rank in the "genius zone." You love life to be in order. It is reassuring to know that you are someone who will do what you say—a woman of your

word. I'm sure your teachers love you, because you love to learn. You're a perfectionist about your schoolwork.

❝You love life to be in order.❞

I purposely surround myself with Thelma Thinkers. I know that I can count on them to keep me organized.

I have a very precious friend who is a Thelma Thinker. She amazes me—even her closet is a work of art. Let me give you an example. Her hangers are all the same color, and each pair of her shoes is in a plastic Tupperware container, stacked in perfect order and color-coded. Her clothes are more color coordinated than the color wheel. There is nothing on the floor in her closet, and she knows where everything is.

She is great at planning and sticking to a schedule. My Thelma Thinker friend and I took a trip to Sea World together. As soon as we stepped foot in the park, she grabbed a list of show times and a map of Sea World. In just a few minutes she had written out a chart showing how long we could stay at each attraction, including how long it would take to walk from each place in the park. Then she set her watch to the exact same time as the "Shamu Clock" at Sea World "to make sure we were not off by a second."

Now that she had created our day with the perfect plan, we could start having fun. I'll never forget her reaction when I wanted to stop and take a picture with the dolphins. I thought she would deactivate and her brain was going to blow up. "If you wanted to take pictures, you should have put it in the sched-ule," she told me.

"Just flash the camera, and we can run to the next attraction

> **"** *You were created to set the standard of excellence and keep the world in order.* **"**

to make up lost time," I suggested. Believe it or not, she made me run through the park to get back to her schedule of fun!

YOU GO, GIRL!

Your future is full of potential because you have so much natural talent. Your greatest challenge will be deciding where to invest your great gift. You could be a great surgeon, office manager, scientist, music artist, writer, teacher or creator of anything that requires attention to detail. Your list of opportunities is open to whatever you decide to invest your time and talent into. You will go far in life if you learn to live with life's interruptions.

Not everything will go as you have planned, but for the most part, you can count on order in your private world—even when the world around you seems to be out of control. Remember that just as God created you to organize and analyze, He gifted your other friends and family members with specific talents also. It's Debbie Doer who gets us going. Terri Talker makes us lighten up and laugh. And Pamela Peacemaker helps us to be comfortable and content.

However, I must give all you Thelma Thinkers a word of caution: Not everyone is wired like you! Be careful not to use your talent to tear down others with your critical comments. If you do, others may accuse you of being the president of the

"Creative Criticizers of America Club." You were created to set the standard of excellence and keep the world in order. That's incredible. So do it! But there's a difference between *caring* and *criticizing.*

Also, don't be so hard on yourself; as good as you are at living life the right way, remember that none of us are perfect. You may be closest to perfect as a Thelma Thinker, because you try the hardest to conquer perfection. But the other side of that is that you are also the hardest on yourself. In other words, do your best; let God perfect the rest.

I encourage you to use your great talent to touch others, not tear them down just because they are not as naturally organized as you are. I also give you a word of caution about criticism: People will welcome your perfectionism much better if you learn to demonstrate it with love. Your deep detail dynamic is great because you see the whole puzzle of life, small pieces and all! We need someone with your talent to take account of the small important pieces of life that really do matter.

We are all needed as stars up on the "Stage of Life." Without each person's unique gifts and characteristics, the "Show of Life" would not be a complete success.

Let's Talk About Patient Pamela Peacemaker

Everybody loves Pamela Peacemaker. Of course they do; what's not to love? You are the closest thing to being an angel on earth. Your talent to touch others with love and acceptance is such a blessing. You hear the heartbeat of everyone who knows you.

My very best friend is a Pamela Peacemaker. She calms my

> **" You hear the heartbeat of everyone who knows you. "**

spirit, laughs at my jokes and cares for my complex life. I thank God for a friend who is patient, kind and forgiving. She brings peace into my world, even though there is an endless list of things she has endured to be my friend.

One story exceeds them all. Pamela Peacemaker and I were roommates when I was single. Pamela does not like conflict, and she always runs to the rescue of a hurting heart. At one point, I was in a conflict with my boyfriend, and I could not sleep. One night I decided to write him a letter and take the letter to his apartment and tape it to his door—at 2:00 A.M.

As I sat in my bed, the thought came to me, "I should get Pamela Peacemaker out of her cozy, warm bed and drag her to the car in the freezing cold so she can help me conquer this conflict with my boyfriend." Off I went up the stairs to her bedroom. There she lay, sleeping so peacefully. There I sat, at the end of her bed crying out of control.

Of course she woke up to comfort me because that's what Pamela Peacemakers do best. She said five dangerous words (dangerous to a desperate Terri Talker): "How can I help you?"

Bless her heart! I don't think she was prepared for my request. "I want you to drive with me to my boyfriend's house so I can tape this letter on his door before he wakes up." She got out of bed, exhausted out of her mind, put on her robe and slippers and said, "Let's go and get this over with so we can both get some sleep." We drove to his house and parked in his driveway. I turned off the car and took the keys without thinking to leave the heat on for Pamela. To make matters worse, the window was stuck down on her side of the car.

When I walked up to his doorway to tape the note to the door, he heard me and came outside. We hadn't spoken in weeks, so it was an awkward moment—not to mention that it was now about 3:30 A.M. He read the letter while I stood there, and then invited me to come in and talk about it.

"Well, OK," I answered. "But only for a minute." As we talked inside, I felt so relieved that our friendship was being reconciled that I completely forgot that Pamela was still in the car in her robe and slippers.

Now you might be wondering why Pamela didn't just knock on the door and say, "Let's go home." Well, a Doberman pincher had taken care of that. The minute I walked inside, the Doberman that belonged to the policeman next door came charging over to the half-open car window to eat my best friend for a late-night snack. She couldn't roll up the window because it was electric, and I had the key—and besides, it was stuck! She couldn't honk because my horn was broken. All she could do was sit there, frozen in fear, just like a deer caught in head-lights—with only slippers on her feet.

After what seemed like only a few minutes to me, my boyfriend and I had worked everything out. It wasn't until he opened the front door—and I saw my car with a bare-fanged Doberman snout poked in the passenger window as far as it would go—that I remembered I had left Pamela in the car. I looked at my watch. She had been sitting there, inches from being a doggie treat, for three hours!

My boyfriend could not believe it. "I've heard of leaving your keys in your car," he quipped, "but your best friend...?" Anyone

" Turn your fear into prayer. "

else would never have forgotten or *forgiven* my total lack of consideration. But not patient Pamela. All she wanted to do was to pick up where she'd left off—under her fluffy down comforter.

YOU GO, GIRL!

You are dependable and predictable. We can always count on you to care for others and do what you say you will do. No doubt you could stop a world war with your amazing ability to calm and avoid unnecessary conflict. You would make a great counselor, politician, business assistant, psychologist, mediator and, of course, a great wife, because you will faithfully stand by your man and help him climb the ladder to success.

Pamela Peacemaker, you remind the rest of us that life is not just about *us*. You are rarely in a conflict, because you avoid confrontation as much as possible. Pushy people with power are your biggest pet peeve, because they rock your world. You like life to be consistent, calm and without conflict.

Don't get pushed out of shape when Debbie Doer takes control because that's what God created her to do. Just as you were created to calm down situations, she was created to get things going. Thelma Thinker may be a perfectionist, but she also keeps us on the right track. Terri Talker may never let you get a word in, but she'll keep you entertained.

Just remember not to live your life in fear. Learn to look to God. Turn your fear into prayer. Then let go and trust Him to handle with care those things you are concerned about. Everyone who knows you will be blessed by your gift, which you give away without worry about how others will receive it! Remember that not all of us are as calm, cool and comforting as you are. Don't take it personally when we don't react to life the way you do.

When we're going through problems in our lives, it's easy to get so wrapped up in ourselves that we overlook the Pamelas God brings along to help us through. In a world where everyone wants his own way, Pamela Peacemaker still sets the standard for self-less living.

However, I have a word of caution for you, also. Life can be hard. Sometimes the only way back to your "place of peace" is to cross over a "rocky road." But remember that running from the rat race won't get rid of the rats.

I have a friend who loves to volunteer for any and all meaningful ministries. She is a blessing when she comes in to lend a helping hand. But when trouble hits and she gets hurt, she silently exits the scene, never to return. She has a closet full of unresolved conflicts. Don't leave any situation without letting people learn from your pleasant personality. Remember that hiding your hurts won't heal your heart. We need you to be happy and healthy so you can help others—which, by the way, you love to do! So do it!

Closing the Show

Isn't it fun to discover your talent? Maybe you've even discovered that you're multitalented. Many of us are a combination of two of the personalities we've talked about.

Remember that it takes many characters to produce a movie. Learn from others by watching how they perform. Prepare for your audition by understanding what role is best for you and then practicing how you play that role. Before the "Movie of Life" will be a blockbuster success, each player must play her part to the best of her ability.

The Author of Life, God Himself, has created each character. He's the scriptwriter, the producer and the director of the "Movie of Life." He did not forget your part, but perhaps you have lost the script.

Don't select your part by what others say. Many of us are capable of playing many parts. Because we are influenced by our friends and families' reactions toward us, we often do not know what our true character is. For example, Terri Talker could be a counselor, but it would not be the best part in the movie of life because she does not like to listen for long. Pamela Peacemaker is very capable of speaking in front of an audience, but deep down she dreads being in front of people. Thelma Thinker can live in the "wing-it" world, but she doesn't enjoy it. Debbie Doer could stop giving people free advice, but it would make her crazy after just a day.

It's very important to discover the true you—not who you think you should be or what others try to make you. The best way to discover if you are performing the perfect part is to pay close attention to how you feel while you are performing in real-life situations. Pay attention to what comes naturally to you! God the Director/Producer would not give you a part to play at which you could not "be yourself."

If you want to find out more about the "true you," I highly recommend the book *Personality Plus* (the revised edition) by

Florence Littauer.[1] In the meantime, practice your part until you've perfected it.

Play the part God designed just for you—because we need you to complete the picture.

GOD TALKS
Movies

God Is...the Producer and Director of Life

God's character acted out through you is the real "Oscar Trophy" worth winning because it's a powerful performance that changes people's lives. So keep practicing your talent with your heart, and memorize your lines in the Script (the Bible). If you take your role in God's movie of life seriously, you will be the spotlight in someone's darkness. You will be the star that points to heaven. You will be the director who instructs a lost soul back to God, and you'll be the audience for someone who needs to be applauded for his or her performance.

Don't wait for the right part to come to you. Play your part every day so that when the Producer calls you will be ready.

Dear God, help me to cast all my cares and insecurities on You, so You can cast me in Your movie of life. Let me be the character You created me to be.

I am the LORD your God, who teaches you what is best for you, who directs you in the way you should go.

—ISAIAH 48:17

Are you **SURE** you're ready for the roller coaster?

Chapter Three

Girlfriend Talk

If you are anything like me, you love amusement parks. One of my favorite places on earth, really, is amusement parks! I love the attractions, the wild rides and, of course, the food! Girlfriends are kind of like an amusement park experience. Friends can be fun, exciting, exhausting, overwhelming and wild. Sometimes we forget how to ride our relationships the right way. That's why I decided to take you to *Girlfriendland*. So get on your comfy clothes and walking shoes, grab a girlfriend and let's adventure together through some main attractions that will change the way you see yourself and your girlfriends forever.

Relational Roller Coaster

Our first stop is the Relational Roller Coaster. This ride will make you laugh, scream and, of course, will turn you upside down. Before you get in line for the ride, I need you to read the following:

> **R**—Ride with care.
> **U**—Understand that we all react differ-
> ently to the ride.
> **L**—Learn from each other's reactions.
> **E**—Expect more from you than your
> friends.
> **S**—Stay close during the ups and
> downs.

Now that you've read the rules, let's get in line together and wait our turn to take the most important ride of our lives, the Relational Roller Coaster.

If you have ever experienced being a friend, you've found out that it is a lot of work. But it's worth the ticket price to learn how to ride out our differences. Sometimes we get on the ride with great anticipation of how fun and exciting our new friend will be. But many times we discover that the twists and turns are more than we can handle, and we feel a little sick or scared. Just like on a real roller coaster, we need to be ready for the ride.

So let's get on the ride and hang on during the twists and turns. I've had a lot of great girlfriends whom I love and cherish. But not one of my friendships has been a smooth ride. It takes time to learn how to respond, relate and respect the Relational Roller Coaster. I've known some very challenging friends. (By challenging, I mean I wish these people would get deported to another country so I wouldn't have to deal with them at all!) OK, now that the truth is out, let's get back to our talk. Real friends are worth the time it takes to enjoy this attraction. Let's go back and define the rules in detail.

R—Ride with care.

Relationships are only fun and fulfilling if we really care for each other—not just with our words. It is not enough to merely say you care with your mouth. You need to back up your words with your actions.

> **It's not enough to merely say you care with your mouth.**

Do you really care about your relationships, or are you in it for a free ride? Quiz yourself and find out how you score:

Care *quiz*

1. My friend is stressed out about passing a final test. I…

   a) Invite her to come over and help her study, then call the next day to find out how she did.

   b) Tell her not to worry, and then talk her into blowing it off and going out.

2. My friend is bummed out about her weight. I…

   a) Offer to diet and exercise with her for the next month and tell her she's beautiful no matter what she weighs.

   b) Tell her to stop weighing herself and to throw out the scale.

3. My friend has to do a bunch of chores before we can go out to the mall. I....

   a) Offer to come over and help so we can go together.

   b) Tell her I'll meet her at the mall because I don't want to wait.

Total As _____—You are the "real deal." You are someone who truly cares about the relational ride. Your friends are blessed to ride with you. Keep up the heart work!

Total Bs _____—If you answered any of the Bs you will not enjoy the Relational Roller Coaster ride because you don't care with your actions. Anyone can say they care, but a real friend shows it. So get back in line and ride with care.

_____

U—Understand that we all react differently to the ride.

I used to think that if my friends were not smiling and laughing 24/7, they must not want to ride with me. That's not true. We all need to get in the line of life and ride with a friend. But, as we talked about in the talent search in chapter two, we respond differently.

If we put Terri Talker on the roller coaster, she would talk to everyone around her waiting in line. Even if they did not want to talk, they would be forced to listen, because she would be laughing as loud as she talks. She would probably respond to the ride with excitement and fun.

Next in line would be Debbie Doer. Now Debbie would push people down without realizing it, just to get to the front car because it's the most adventurous place on the ride. She would put her hands up the whole time. She likes the thrill of not hanging on to anything, as opposed to Terri who would probably hang on to the poor person's head in front of her, not realizing she was interrupting his ride.

Thoughtful Thelma would be watching the ride to make sure it's safe. Maybe while she was waiting, she would quietly time how long the ride takes, and she would look around to see whom she would be riding with.

Last but not least, Patient Pamela would enjoy watching everyone who went before her on the ride and enjoying all their reactions.

All of us would enjoy the roller coaster in different ways, and we would all react differently to the ups and downs and twists and turns. *Different* doesn't mean we can't ride together.

L—Learn from each other's reactions.

More exciting than accepting the different ways we respond is what we can learn from watching each other. I have learned so much from watching Debbie Doer. She's taught me to work before I play, to be more direct and to take control of my time. Thoughtful Thelma has helped me to learn how to organize my schedule and to think before I speak, and Patient Pamela has taught me to be a better listener. Your friends are put on your relational ride for a reason. Don't miss out on the excitement of growing together.

> **" A true friend knows all your ups and downs, but she stays on the ride with you anyway. "**

E—Expect more from you than your friends.

In other words, don't put pressure on your friends to lift you in the car so you can enjoy the ride. So many times we expect our friends to do all the work in the relationship. We want them to be the one to call or to make all the plans. If they don't, we push them out of our line of friendship—and that's not right. So many girls feel alone because they just sit on the bench by the Relational Roller Coaster, refusing to get on and ride with someone unless the other person does all the work. If you want to ride, then get off your seat. Take a seat next to someone who needs a friend as much as you do!

S—Stay close during the ups and downs.

Too many of us get off the ride when a relationship gets rough. Remember we all blow it. We all say things that hurt each other or do things that disappoint each other. You'll never find anyone who does the right relational thing every single time. A true friend knows all your ups and downs, but she stays on the ride with you anyway.

My very best friend of many years has seen me at my worst. She has forgiven me for forgetting her birthday, for forgetting her in a car with a Doberman pincher outside the window, for forgetting to meet her at the mall—the list is endless of the things for which she has forgiven me and seen me through. But it's those things that give her the title of "Best Friend."

Stick close during the relational ride, or you will miss out on the memories that last a lifetime.

Gabby Go-carts

Our next stop in Girlfriendland is Gabby Go-carts. So grab a go-cart, and let's learn to run our mouths in the right direction. Our words, as we talked about in chapter one (beautiful lips), can make our relationships crash on the course or can help us to react to win our friends' hearts. If you learn the track, it will be worth your entire ticket price to get into Girlfriendland. So let's race to win! As always, before you get into the go-cart, we need to read the rules.

R—Race your mouth to win friends.
U—Understand the track of your tongue.
L—Learn when to shut down your Gabby Go-cart.
E—Every time you gossip, you'll get off track.
S—Say the right thing.

R—Race your mouth to win friends.

Save your competition for the sports field where people want to watch you win. In Girlfriendland, we don't care about winning our way if we lose our friends. I've watched a lot of girls gab to get their way rather than gab to give a girlfriend a word of encouragement.

Our Gabby Go-carts can cause people to hide so they won't have to ride with us. Don't waste your thirty-thousand-plus words a day by trying to prove your point, get your way, talk out of turn or bring bad news.

Have you ever met someone who caused you to cringe every time they talked? I have. It was a girl at our school who was on the cheerleading team. When she was in front of an audience, she had lots of energy and a big smile, and she yelled victory cheers enthusiastically. But when the game was over, Little Miss Cheerleader turned into Big Miss Downer, and I'm not talking touchdowns.

It did not matter what anyone said, she always had something bad or sad to say or something sick to share with the group. Eventually everyone started to avoid her. One day I saw her crying out of control in the bathroom. I asked her how I could help.

"Find me some friends who are not so negative and mean!" she told me. I could not believe that she could not see how her own lips were making her lose friends. So I shared with her some winning ways to win her friends back.

If you want to know how well you race your mouth, then pay attention to how people respond to you after you talk. In other words, read the caution signs while you are running your mouth; then slow down long enough to learn from the other drivers on your track. That way, you'll win friends.

U—Understand the track of your tongue.

A smart race driver studies the track so that he can master every turn. You would be amazed at what you can learn about the track of your tongue—if you pay attention to how you drive your mouth. Most of us cause our own problems with our words.

There is a great power behind our motor mouths, but power is dangerous if you don't know how to handle it.

"Sometimes silence speaks louder than words."

I used to cut people off constantly when they were talking. It was not because I didn't care about what they were saying. It was actually for the opposite reason. I was so into what they were talking about that I'd race to ride and finish their sentences for them. I did not realize I was cutting off friendships by cutting into their conversations until one day a good friend said, "Sheri Rose, please stop cutting me off. Let me complete at least one sentence."

I asked her if I always did that, and she yelled, "Yes, and I hate it!" Even though I felt terrible about the truth, it made me understand the track of my tongue. It's been ten years since that happened, and I still have to work on my mouth racing so I don't cut off my precious friends.

L—Learn when to shut down your Gabby Go-cart.

Sometimes silence speaks louder than words. When we don't know what to say, it's better to say nothing at all. As you know, I'm a speaker, generally speaking, so I'm generally speaking. I also have a passion to encourage people who are depressed or hurting. In my mind, the idea of silence means that something is not right. It never dawned on me that some people like quiet, peaceful moments. It seemed too simple just to listen and not respond with words.

One day I was visiting a young teenager in the hospital who

was dying of leukemia. I was so deeply saddened by this experience that I just sat there in silence, along with the young girl's mom. I stayed for hours without words. I wanted desperately to say something that would encourage this mom who was watching her daughter disintegrate before her eyes. But nothing came out. That evening when I went to leave, the mom said, "You will never know how much you helped me just by being here next to me. No one else would come because they didn't know how to respond."

I learned a powerful lesson that day. Just being by someone's side in a crisis is enough. We can be friends without our mouths going around the track continually.

E—Every time you gossip, you'll get off track.

If one of your friends gossips to you about others, I can guarantee they will gossip about you. Gossip is different than gabbing. Gossip is sharing information that hurts someone's reputation or causes someone to think badly about the person you're gossiping about. Take a minute to think about how you feel about yourself after you race your mouth with harmful words and comments. You feel like you've fallen off the track, because no one likes a gossip. They may listen to your trash, but they won't help you pick it up.

Before you share personal or inaccurate information about another person, ask yourself the following questions:

1. Why am I sharing this information?

2. How will it benefit the person listening?

3. Am I willing to let my name be used as a reference when someone repeats what I'm sharing?

4. How would the person feel if she were standing next to me while I was gossiping about her?

> **"Get a tune-up on your tongue."**

Even if a friend or stranger gossips about you, don't get even by getting ugly. Your true character will eventually win the race against your reputation.

If the answer is not positive to any of the questions above, don't gossip and get off track. Nothing will make a friendship blow up faster than gossip, so get a tune-up on your tongue. Remember, even if the gossip is true, it's the wrong way to go.

S—Say the right thing.

Saying the right thing at the right time is a guaranteed win. You will win respect, trust and honor just by practicing your performance. Before we leave this ride on the Gabby Go-carts, I want to give you a list of "right things to say." Take this list with you as a souvenir:

Thank you.
Please.
How can I help?
I appreciate you.
How are you feeling today?
Is this a good time to talk?
I'm so glad to see you today.
I know you can do it.
You're special to me.

I'm blessed to be your friend.
I would love to do that for you.
Don't worry; God is in control.
How can I pray for you today?

This is a list that says, "You are important enough for me to say the right thing." When you say it, you'll feel it, and so will your friends.

Argue Arcade

Our next stop is the ever-so-popular attraction "Argue Arcade." So many friends and families argue away their love for each other, and they're not winning any prizes for their punch. Most of us don't want to argue, but anger happens, so how do we learn to play the game in the Argue Arcade? Let's start with the rules.

R—Refuse to lose it.
U—Unfinished fights don't fix it.
L—Learn to let go.
E—Excuses don't win a prize.
S—Say you're sorry.

R—Refuse to lose it.

My dad used to say to me, "Don't win the battle and lose the war." Those were winning words of wisdom to live by. Who cares if a small battle is won if a big major war is lost? The best way to win is to let the other person do the dirty fighting. Keep yourself clean. Losing it is for losers, and you're a winner.

Winners stop arguments before they begin. How do you do that? Believe me, there is a way to win your argument without losing your friends.

First, listen to what the other person has to say before you jump in the ring with your boxing gloves on.

Next, thank the person for being truthful; then pray hard for the person to hear your heart and for words of wisdom. You can say anything if you learn to say it with the right attitude.

Most importantly: If you feel you're about to lose it, leave the Argue Arcade immediately, and don't return until you're ready to play fair. When I'm upset and don't know what to do, I don't do anything. So often we say and do something while we are upset that we regret later. It's better to swallow your angry words than to have to eat them later.

Last, but not least, try to remember that we all lose it sometimes. So don't be so hard on yourself or your friend when it happens.

U—Unfinished fights don't fix it.

Spending your time at the Argue Arcade is not any fun. But unfinished fights can finish off a friendship forever. So play the game until you both win an understanding or agreement. Sometimes you will need to agree to disagree in order to finish a fight.

I have many friends who see things totally different than I do. They do things I disagree with. (I am not talking about immoral things.) I'm talking about the way my friends deal with their personal issues and the way I deal with mine. But I love my friends, and I don't want to dump our friendships just because we see things differently. Besides, if two of you agree

> **Character in friendships is just as important as comfort in friendships.**

on everything, there is only need for one of you! So fight for the friendship, and win the big stuffed prize at the Argue Arcade.

L—Learn to let go.

When arguments happen between girlfriends, it's a great opportunity to learn more about your friend's likes and dislikes. It's an even better time to learn about yourself. *Character* in friendships is just as important as *comfort* in friendships.

I used to always be late when meeting my friends. I always had a legitimate reason for my tardiness. But one day, my good friend got tired of "waiting time," so she took off before I got to the mall to meet her. She didn't call me on my cell phone or leave a message at my apartment. I was really worried—and mad—about sitting there with nothing to do but wait.

When I finally reached her two hours later, I told her that I had been waiting and waiting. "Where were you?" I asked.

"I'm not going to make plans with you ever again," she replied. "I'm so tired of your tardiness." I knew she was mad.

"I don't blame you for how you feel," I told her. "I finally understand how it feels to sit and wait for two hours for me."

Sometimes life's lessons are only learned through misunderstandings or when people get mad at us. Instead of leaving and giving up, learn to let go of the bad experience, and hold on to the helpful lesson you learned.

E—Excuses don't win a prize.

Excuses are the nails that build a house of failure. Excuses never fix a fight. When someone is upset with us, and we don't understand why that person is mad, it's only natural to make excuses. "You don't know what you're talking about." Or, "It's not that bad." Or, "I can't help it."

If we dig deep in our excuse backpacks, we can always find some reason why we are right and the person upset at us is wrong. But what do we really win with an excuse? We don't win back a friendship or heal someone's hurting heart. Who cares how good your excuse is if you lose the game of life.

Let me give you an illustration that may help you to understand people's pain. If you run over someone's foot with a Razor scooter, whether on purpose or by accident, the pain is still the same to that person you hurt. So stop wasting your time building a house of failure with excuses. Build a strong foundation for your friendships by accepting responsibility for running over their hearts.

S—Say you're sorry.

It sounds simple, but it's not. It takes a very special talent to tell someone you're sorry. Anyone can say the words, but real friends say it with their actions. What I'm trying to say is this: Do what it takes until that person knows you're really serious about this sorry business.

For example, I wanted my friend who was sick of me for being late all the time to know how sorry I really was, so I acknowledged her feelings instead of excusing my tardiness. Then I wrote her a letter and enclosed a gift certificate to her

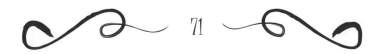

❝ People cannot make you feel inferior or insecure without your permission! ❞

favorite restaurant. I even offered to pick her up.

I showed up thirty minutes early so she would know I really was sorry and that she was important enough for me to be on time in the future. When you blow it, don't just beg forgiveness. Go the extra mile, and make a point of proving that you really are sorry.

People Mover Ride

This is the most powerful ride in Girlfriendland, so get on with caution. I want to teach you how to hang on to your heart and use your head while you are on the ride, because nothing robs your fun faster than being on this ride with the wrong people.

You can have more fun doing nothing with the right friends than by being at your favorite place with the wrong friends. Let's start with some truth: People cannot make you feel inferior or insecure without your permission!

> **R**—Remove yourself from people
> who bring you down.
> **U**—Understand how your friends
> affect you.
> **L**—Look for a lifeguard.
> **E**—Enjoy the ride guilt free.
> **S**—Stay strong in your convictions.

R—Remove yourself from people who bring you down.

Friends are like buttons on an elevator—they can take you up or bring you down. Surround yourself with people who are like what you want to become, because you become like those with whom you surround yourself. When I left elementary school, we moved to Sacramento, where I attended junior high school. Then we moved again, this time to San Jose while I was in high school. I was desperate for friends. I never gave a thought to who those friends were or what they acted like. I just wanted to be liked by somebody. I wanted to be invited to do the things others were doing. Unfortunately, I began hanging out with the "it's-cool-to-be-crude" crowd. Within one year after I joined this crowd, I started being rude to my dad and my stepmom. I started swearing, smoking and getting stoned every day before school. I gained weight, started dressing like a dirty, "I-don't-care" slob, and my happy heart turned into a hard heart.

The weird thing is that I did not notice how much I had changed until I saw that "Kodak picture" I talked about at the beginning of this book. One stupid choice at a time, choice after choice, can change you into a person you don't want to be. However, one good choice at a time, choice after choice, can change you into a better girl than you ever dreamed possible. So choose to hang out in the right circle of friends.

YOU GO, GIRL!

Write down the names of all your friends on a piece of paper. Then write down what kind of person each friend is and how you feel about yourself when you're with them.

Invite someone you trust to tell you honestly what he or she thinks about your choices for friends. Don't get defensive when that person gives you the answers—just get smart, listen and learn.

Don't chance experiencing anything just to please your friends. One wrong experience at the wrong time can unplug your power to win what you really want out of life.

U—Understand how your friends affect you.

If you want to know how the people in your world affect you, take this test: The next time you spend a day with one of your chosen friends, pay attention to how you feel about yourself and your family when you leave your friend. If you discover you feel bummed out or burnt out emotionally, you might want to take back the power to choose your friends. Make a power play and choose to exit out of that friendship for a while. Many of us get stuck in a relationship rut that zaps the excellence right out of us.

L—Look for a lifeguard.

Everyone needs a lifeguard—and I'm not talking about a blond beach babe. I'm talking about a buddy to hold you up when the waters get rough. Today's waters are more than rough—they are life threatening. There are hungry sharks clamoring to take a bite out of our minds, bodies and souls. They want to wash us up with dirty water, dirty drugs and dirty jokes so they can drown our hopes and dreams. If you think I'm being a drama queen, check out these statistics:

- ❀ Nearly four in ten young women become pregnant at least once before they reach the age of twenty—nearly one million a year.[1]

- More than one million youth ages twelve through seventeen are dependent on illicit drugs.[2]

- Teenagers are infected with HIV at an average rate of more than one an hour, according to a new report released by the White House Office of AIDS Policy. [3]

- Half of all students have had sex by the end of high school.[4]

- Every twenty-five seconds, someone under eighteen runs away from home.[5]

- More than 26,000 gangs, with more than 840,500 gang members, were estimated to be active in the United States in 1999.[6]

- An estimated 46 percent of youth gang members are involved in street drug sales to generate profit for the gang.[7]

I don't mean to be drastic, but I want you to get a grip on reality and learn to guard your life for your protection. Learn to stay within the safe waters of our world by following the principles we just talked about. Even if you find yourself in the same waters with the sharks, you don't have to let them take you down.

E—Enjoy the ride guilt free.

Once you set your heart and mind on a goal or dream, don't look back. My dear friend Lisa Bevere says, "Your past is not your future." Many of us don't set goals because we are insecure or afraid of failing. That's OK, as long as you turn your fear into faith to finish what you started.

> **Once you set your heart and mind on a goal or dream, don't look back.**

When I was participating in my first Miss California Pageant and heard all the other contestants at rehearsals talking about their GPAs, community involvement, great families and accomplishments, I thought to myself, *What am I doing here? I don't fit in. I'll never win.*

Just then my dad came up to me and said, "You have come so far from your past, Sheri Rose. I am so proud of you." His words helped to keep me going toward my goal. Maybe I did not have all the same things the other girls had, but I did want to win for the right reasons—not to prove I was beautiful or to have people worship me. I wanted to help people see through me that they could conquer anything, no matter what was in their way.

By the way, I did not win for five years. Finally, because I did not give up, I think the judges got so sick of seeing me that they picked me to win. But even if I had never won a crown, I still won the war over failure from my past. My purpose for being in the pageant kept me strong enough to see the win from a different perspective.

This message is not just about me—this is about *you*. Let go of anything that gets in your way of being the best version of you. Release anything that holds you back from going after your goals.

S—Stay strong in your convictions.

If all your friends were running in the dark to the top of a mountain with a two-hundred-foot cliff on the other side, would you run with them? Many of your friends are running toward a mountaintop experience, only to find there is a cliff on the other side. They don't want to fall off the cliff, but they do want to live life on the edge of it. Many people fall off and fail just because they ran with the crowd—and that crowd had no idea where it was running.

During my senior year of high school, our beautiful homecoming queen decided to walk on the wild side on homecoming night. Before the homecoming, she never drank, smoked or went to the wrong parties. But on this night our homecoming king talked her into experiencing "life on the edge." She chose to drink along with him and their other friends in the homecoming court.

She discovered that she liked the feeling of being tipsy from a little alcohol, so she drank even more, and so did he. While our king was driving our queen to their homecoming—both of them a little drunk—he swerved onto the wrong side of the road and hit a car carrying a mother and her young children head-on at fifty miles per hour. The young family was killed, and the homecoming queen flew through the window because she was not wearing her seat belt. Her first-time walk on the wild side took her through a windshield. She did not die, but she was cut up and scarred severely all over her face and body. To this day she walks with a cane.

I'm sure that every time she looks at her scarred reflection in the mirror, she reflects on the one night when she gave in and lost her grip.

It's not worth "just one time." Get a grip, and don't ever give in to a walk on the wild side. There are countless stories about

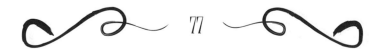

> **Laughter is the medicine to our souls and the music of our memories.**

young people who would give anything to get back their grip and get it right.

Giggle House of Fun

Our final destination of the day at Girlfriendland is the Giggle House of Fun. This is my favorite place, because I love to laugh with my friends. As you know, I have a silly sense of humor. I believe laughter is the medicine to our souls and the music of our memories. So let's giggle and grow together.

Before we go into the Giggle House, we have to learn to laugh at ourselves. We all have embarrassing times or say silly things, and it's great to be able to laugh and let go of those awkward moments. So get a grip on the Giggle House rules.

R—Remember to smile.
U—Unless you laugh, you'll lose it.
L—Lose the sarcasm.
E—Exit out of Dumpsville.
S—Sayings that only girls get.

R—Remember to smile.

Life can seem too stressful to smile. I once read a bumper sticker that said, "Life stinks…then you die!" First of all, what kind of person publicizes in writing that their life is awful? Yes, life can stink, and so can relationships. But you would be shocked to know the impact a simple smile has on a world full of "pouty people."

I put this smile thing to the test and had nearly a 98 percent return rate. There is something about a smile that people can't resist, no matter how hard their hearts are. A smile warms the world up to you. A smile changes the way people treat you. A smile gets you the extra mile you need to get to the destination of the day. A smile places you above the rest. A smile is free to give, but worth a lot to the person receiving it. So don't poop out when life stinks; pick up your lips and smile.

U—Unless you laugh, you'll lose it.

I had to learn to laugh at myself. I've done many klutzy things—from falling off a beauty pageant stage to dumping spinach salad on a bald man's head. And that's just a few of the many memory builders I've shared with you. I've also said some wild whoppers that have left people in the audience in shock. Thank God I know how to use laughter to dig myself out of the Giggle Ground Holes I've got myself into. I love saying it just like it is, but that once got me really stuck in a "crazy crack."

I was hosting a nationally televised model search. My job was to use my mouth to keep the show moving smoothly. The producers there actually put their trust in me to announce each model and describe each outfit accurately. Talking is my talent, and details are my downfall. But I like challenges and new experiences, so I took the responsibility of hosting the show.

When I got there, I was so freaked out about reading the names correctly aloud that I didn't notice the heels of my shoes were sliding down in the crack between the stage risers. Suddenly the lights were on, the TV show began and they

announced my name. That was my cue to walk out and greet the audience, but I was stuck! Both heels of my shoes were lodged in the cracks. I panicked, said into the live microphone, "Can someone come set me free? My heels are stuck in my crack!"

I realized how stupid that sounded and burst out laughing. So did the audience. Finally someone ran backstage, sawed off my heels and set me free to finish the show.

In that case, laughter helped me to keep my job as a host. Sometimes a good laugh is the best Band-Aid to an awkward situation.

L—Lose the sarcasm.

Giggle House is for all to have fun. Having fun by making fun of someone by using sarcasm, pranks or anything that causes pain is the wrong way to play at the Giggle House.

Has anyone ever played a joke on you that hurt your heart or ruined your fun? We all love to play around, but don't blow someone out of the water with a big splash of sarcastic fun.

Let's talk about the difference between silly and sarcasm. *Silly* is a funfest for everyone. A good laugh is at something everyone can relate to. Doing something silly with your friend— like walking around town with green beauty mud masks on your face—can give you a good laugh. But *sarcasm* is the complete opposite of silly. Sarcasm is when we say something stupid about someone else, causing everyone to laugh except the person who is the brunt of the joke.

Sarcasm can also be a mean prank we play, one that hurts or embarrasses another person. Some friends and family members played a prank on me at my thirtieth birthday that I will never forget. For some girls, turning thirty would be a bad deal. But I love life so much, and I act so silly, that I never think about my age. But I've thought about this one a lot.

> ❝ Try taking a vacation from your negative attitude. ❞

It was 10:00 P.M. I was getting ready for bed when all the lights went out and the house went black inside. Now very few things scare me, but being in the dark alone totally freaks me out. As I stumbled in the dark, feeling my way to the front door so I could get outside to the electric box, I smashed my leg on the coffee table, cutting it badly.

After ten minutes of pain, I managed to push my way to the front door. As I gathered the courage to open it, there stood some friends and family members in black clothes holding candles and a cardboard tombstone with my name on it. They were cracking up, but I burst into tears and ran inside.

The unfortunate thing about sarcasm and pranks is that most of us don't do them to hurt someone we love. We do it just for fun. I learned to lose the sarcastic jokes and keep my memories with my friends and family pain-free!

E—Exit out of Dumpsville.

Sometimes we need to dump our worries and do something fun. When I feel overwhelmed about life, I find someone to go with me to have a Giggle House experience. I meet people when I speak who say they have not laughed or had fun in years. I've watched high school girls waste their lives picking up other people's "trash," then go dump it on friends and family.

It's impossible to have clean fun in the sun if you never exit out of Dumpsville. Try taking a vacation from your negative attitude. Perk up some positive energy and learn to laugh a little. If you're always down, you might want to break free from some of the negative forces you're allowing in your path. (See chapter six about defeating depression.)

S—Sayings that only girls get.

Don't you love how we girls have our own GirlTalk language? I thought I would leave you with some silly sayings that will give you a good giggle:

- ❀ "You need a break."—Code for, "You are totally losing it, so take a time out and get it together."

- ❀ "Are you sure about that?"—Code for, "I highly doubt you know what you're talking about."

- ❀ "That's interesting."—Code for, "You are sharing some really weird information that I really didn't need to know, but I don't want to make you feel stupid by pointing that out."

- ❀ "It has your name on it."—Code for, "I don't want it, so stop offering it to me."

- ❀ "Can you hear that?"—Code for, "Stop talking so much and let me get a word in edgewise!"

- ❀ "I'll be ready in a minute."—Code for, "I'll be ready after I shower, blow-dry my hair, do my makeup and change outfits five times."

- ❀ "Can you do me a favor?"—Code for, "Stop what you are doing immediately and focus on me now!"

❀ "I'm allergic."—Code for, "Get that food out of my face."

❀ "Let's pig out together."—Code for, "I'm feeling fat so let me help you gain some weight with me."

❀ "It's fine."—Code for, "I want to throw you in a pool of ice-cold water on a winter day for doing that to me!"

❀ A bad hair day"—Code for, "I need you to tell me how awesome my new hair cut looks on me."

❀ "I'm PMSing."—Code for, "I need chocolate!"

These code phrases give you freedom to express yourself without cutting into the fun. It's time to talk about boys next, but I hope you've laughed and learned some things to let your girl-friends get blessed by you. If you follow all the Girlfriendland rules in your relationships, you will become everyone's favorite friend.

You Go, Girl!

Before you leave Girlfriendland, take a moment to tell a friend how you feel about your visit. Make every ride through this chapter again together!

GOD TALKS
Friendships

God Is...the Best Friend

Girlfriendland is great. But there is not a better friend on earth than God Himself. He is the One who walks in when the world walks out. He is strong when we are weak. He is comfort when we need to be calmed. He is protection when we're in trouble. He is the only One who will always say the right thing in His Word. He is the best friend we are looking for. And He is the only One who can make us into the friends we want to be to others.

I always wanted close girlfriends, but I didn't have a lot of girlfriends in high school because I didn't know how to be a friend. Today I have more friends than I have time to spend with them. So what changed? God changed me when I started to pray, "God, make me a good friend." "God, give me the words to say." "God, guard my lips from gossiping." "God, help me to resolve this argument." "God, give me ability to bless my friends."

Don't go to Girlfriendland without allowing God to give you the tour of real friendship.

Dear God, make me into the friend I desire to have.

I no longer call you servants, because a servant does not know his master's business. Instead, I have called you friends, for everything that I learned from my Father I have made known to you.
—JOHN 15:15

Don't waste
your lips on a
LOSER!

Chapter Four

Boy
Talk

So far we've had a lot of fun together. We got our beauty makeovers in chapter one; then we entered a talent search and were cast in the movie of life. We've had a good time touring the attractions at Girlfriendland, but we are not finished yet, because we have not played America's favorite sport—football.

Before we start playing the game, we have to pick what team we want to play on. There are two teams to choose from in the GirlTalk League:

❀ The "Safe Sex" team—the team that teaches you how to lose safely.

❀ The "Pure Play" team—the team that teaches you how to play to win the "Super Bowl Winner's Ring."

So take a seat; it's time for the pep talk. After you've heard the cheer from both teams, you'll have to make a choice. So let's get started with the cheers.

Give Me a C.H.E.E.R. for the "Safe Sex" Team

> **C**—Check out the Impurity Zone.
> **H**—Hand over your heart.
> **E**—Expect to lose respect.
> **E**—Expect pain when you play.
> **R**—Rules were made to be broken.

Team #1–The "Safe Sex" Team

C—Check out the Impurity Zone.

Have you ever heard someone say, "Just this one time won't matter"? Ask the homecoming queen who decided to get drunk and drive with her drunken date if "just once" mattered. Check out the sexual Impurity Zone. "Just once" can affect the rest of your life. The Impurity Zone is not just about sex. It's about playing the game at the wrong end of the field and thinking you're safe.

My father has always told me that the way to get a guy to treat you like a princess is to act like one, and princesses are pure sexually. His wise words worked for a while. But all my friends were playing the game of sex, and it seemed like they enjoyed the game. I felt like I was missing out by refusing to join their game. Temptation, curiosity and peer pressure won, and so I decided to check into the Impurity Zone with a really great boyfriend who I really thought I loved.

Before that one night, we had a winning relationship. We loved hanging out together. But the next day he acted differently toward me. I didn't feel like his princess anymore. I felt dethroned from my special place in his heart. He wasn't just *different*; he was *distant*. I missed my friend—one night was not worth it! I wanted to run out of the Impurity Zone, but I couldn't because I was pregnant.

When my teammate found out, he walked off the field and quit the game of love with me. Not only was I nauseous, emotional and scared out of my wits—I was totally paralyzed by the pain of playing the sex game. I wished I could erase that "one" time—but there were no instant replays! I was frozen in my failure and alone.

I did not know where to go or who could help. My dad would flip out if I told him, so I visited Planned Parenthood hoping they could give me some comfort and coaching. There in the waiting room were ten other pregnant teenagers. I couldn't help wondering if they played their games by using the "just once in the wrong zone" play. But regardless of what plays got us to that point—we were left alone and injured from playing in the Impurity Zone. No one else from that team knew how to help pick us up off the field.

If only the Safe Sex coaches would have told us that *safety* is not guaranteed—it was regret and guilt that were guaranteed if you played the field.

The nurse at Planned Parenthood walked in just as I was replaying in my mind: *One night equals this mess!* She handed each of us a pill to relax us. Before I took the pill, I asked, "Is this baby alive inside of me?"

"Of course not," she told me. "It's just 'a growth' until five months." With that answer I took the pill, and thirty minutes later I was rolled into a room for the doctor to remove the growth.

"When you hand over your heart to a player, he will run with it. "

As soon as I left that place I knew in my heart that I had made another bad play. I had lost my virginity, my boyfriend and now a baby. I was desperate to stop thinking and replaying my poor choices in my mind. So I tried to kill my memory with drugs.

Checking out the Impurity Zone will steal your ball of joy, power and purpose. Maybe you won't get stuck in the same bad position from your first play as I did, but you will lose your ability to win what you really want—a real relationship with a boy who loves you for all the right reasons.

I know I'm hitting you hard on the field, but I want you to do more than play safe. Not only do I want to block you from giving your body and soul to the wrong team—I want you to win. So if I have to be the one to tackle you with the truth, I will. I'm a coach who really cares!

H—Hand over your heart.

The Safe Sex team teaches their players how to protect themselves while they play around in the Impurity Zone. But unfortunately for their players, there is no helmet hard enough or pads thick enough to protect the players' hearts from getting hurt when they give in to the game of Safe Sex.

Many girls on the team play the field, but they think it's safe because they don't go "all the way" into the Impurity Zone. However, there are more reasons not to fool around than merely getting pregnant or contracting a STD (sexually transmitted disease). *What about your heart?* Even holding a guy in your arms and connecting your lips to his can connect your heart. And when you hand over your heart to a player, he will run with it.

After my first play in the Impurity Zone, I committed never again to have sex until I was married. I made it to the Marriage Zone with those winning words of commitment. But while I was practicing on the field of boys,

> **❝ Respect is not something we can demand— it's something we get only when we play by the right rules. ❞**

many times I did not realize that a passionate kiss still left my heart without a guard to protect it. After one too many "heart plays," I decided to save all my body parts, including my lips, for the one man I would play with forever, my husband.

E—Expect to lose respect.

When my mom cautioned me about the playing tactics of some boys, she would tell me, "The attitude of some boys is, 'Why pay for the cow when you can get the milk for free?'" She was a wise player. I'm not calling you a cow, but I am calling you valuable. Respect is not something we can demand—it's something we get only when we play by the right rules.

After my play in the Impurity Zone, I lost all self-respect. People began to treat me differently because I acted differently. Or maybe because so many of us are walking around without self-respect, we don't know how to respect each other. Something changes inside us when we give a piece of ourselves for free. But we can get it back if we switch teams. The Safe Sex team may play safe, but their so-called "protection" cannot protect their reputations or get respect for them from other players.

E—Expect pain when you play.

Safe Sex team players are used to pain—especially the girls on the team. Girls don't play the game with just their bodies; they play it with their hearts. Boys play the game for fun; girls play the game with all they have to give.

Even though they don't want to get pain when they play, it's inevitable, so they learn to live with it. Players on the Safe Sex team often get involved in the win-lose game of love and hate. They want to win—and they love while they think they are winning. But they don't want to experience the pain of losing—so they hate while they are losing.

R—Rules were made to be broken.

The coaches of the Safe Sex team mess with the minds of their players. They bend so many of God's great rules about the game of sex that the team does not know how to play by the rules any longer, so they lose the game. Many of these players lose more than the game. They lose their self-respect and their power and strength to win. They lose their grip on the ball. Even if a girl player tackles a boy's heart with her "safe sex" game tactics, she doesn't know how to hold on to it. So many times that boyfriend wiggles out of her tackle hold and trades that girl off for some new girl player.

Team #2–The "Pure Play" Team

Let's hear the C.H.E.E.R. for the "Pure Play" Team

> **C**—Check out the Pure Power
> Zone.
> **H**—Hold on to your heart.
> **E**—Expect the best.
> **E**—Experience the game in control.
> **R**—Rules are the way to win.

C—Check out the Pure Power Zone.

The Pure Power Zone wins the game every time because you have nothing to lose. Think about it; if a guy dumps you because you won't have sex with him, then he only wanted you for one thing. So you saved yourself tears, time and a tough game of pain on the winner's side of the field.

If the guy you like plays the game by your rules, he's a winner—and so are you! I like holding on to my heart when I play the dating game. I know from personal experience how powerful the Pure Play team is. When I was twenty-four years old, God became my Head Coach. I decided to check out the power of His rules about sex, and they really worked! Almost too well! I liked three different guys who lived in three different cities. I refused to give into the sex game, and within three months, all three of these players had proposed to me in the same week! I had no idea that purity could be so powerful until I put it to the test. To find a good team player, check out the Pure Power Zone.

H—Hold on to your heart.

When I was in my teens and early twenties, I was in love with love. I never cared who the boy was as long as he made all the right moves and said all the right things. I was a loser in the "love game." Using my heart without using my head left me broken most of the time in my young love life.

Maybe you're the same. Do you throw your heart down the football field hoping any player will catch it? That's a dangerous way to play the game. Your heart is your most valuable piece of playing equipment in this game. Guard it by giving attention to how you play. Use your head—don't hold your heart out for anyone to steal. Love is not a game—it's a *gift*.

E—Expect the best.

When I learned how to handle my heart and play the Pure Game, I played the football game expecting to win, and I did every time. I won self-respect. I won self-control. And I won back my confidence.

I love playing on the Pure Play team, because I love to feel like a winner. I love to hear the cheers of my choices.

I didn't marry any of those three guys who proposed to me. I wanted more than a *good* teammate; I wanted the *best* teammate—and that's what I got. My handsome husband is the best. That does not mean we have never experienced some rough plays in our marriage game. But because he's a winner who will never give up or walk away from the game, he's committed to practice until he plays perfectly. That's what I call the best! I've committed to do the same thing.

Any guy can say the right thing and act the right way when

he's in the recruiting mode. But the best player for you is the one who will run with you when life's game gets hard. Wait for the one who is willing to win your heart, *not steal it*!

> *Wait for the one who is willing to win your heart, not steal it!*

E—Experience the game in control.

In football most players get hurt during the game. These injuries can cause pain that lasts a lifetime. But the players on the Pure Play team enjoy the game.

I have played on both teams. When I picked the Pure Play team, I still experienced some pain that comes with the ups and downs of relationships, but I never experienced any pain that could knock me out of the game. If you are guarding your body, you are guarding your heart. So get on the Pure Play team and play your game using the rules of dating and keeping control of your heart.

R—Rules are the way to win.

Before you can be successful at playing any game, you must know the rules. Football coaches spend hours of training time with their players in a classroom where they learn the rules of the game before they ever suit up for the game on the field.

Are you ready to play the game? Do you want to earn your "Super Bowl Winner's Ring" for being a part of the winning team? Then take the time first to learn the following important rules.

Rules for Players in the Super Bowl Game

Rule #1—Lay down the game rules on your first date.

Letting that young man know your boundaries up-front will keep you both from second-guessing what the next play will be. Either he will respect your game, or he will walk off the field. If he walks, he wasn't the right one to play the game with anyway.

Practice talking over your game rules with your girlfriends before you run out on the field. Then when the game starts, you'll know exactly what to say and how to respond to each of your date's reactions. Practice makes perfect!

Rule #2—Invite your friends on your dates.

Taking your friends along with you allows you to watch his "game" and see how he interacts with others before you commit to playing. Then ask your close friends if they saw any weird or negative attitudes or behaviors. Play the game with your eyes open. It hurts when you are blindsided by a ball, even if you have lots of padding!

Rule #3—Get a close-up shot on how he treats women.

Note especially how he treats his own mother and sisters, because that's how he will treat you once the game of dating is over. If a guy treats his mother and sisters the way you want to be treated, you'll want a lifetime of instant replays. If he doesn't, throw that penalty flag down and get off the field.

Rule #4—Avoid being alone on the playing field (translation: "room or car").

Avoiding being alone not only protects you from uncomfortable situations, but it also shows you if he's a true sportsman who doesn't cheat. After you know each other better, only go into his room if you are picking up his dirty laundry as a favor to his mother. Warning: After one whiff of his dirty laundry, you may be tempted to throw a flag and cry, "FOUL!"

Keep the playing field clear—stay in public places and main living areas of your houses, with the doors open. If you do need to have a sideline conversation, try stepping outside to the porch or patio. When you are in his car, don't take any "time-outs" on the side of the road. You both may be tempted to bend your playing rules a bit, which leaves your heart unguarded.

Who cares if he thinks you are unobtainable? That's what keeps you in control of the game and irresistible. You will also avoid the chance of date rape or doing something you'll regret. Besides, he needs to prove he's worth your time and effort. Block his moves, and you'll run a touchdown every time.

Rule #5—Don't intercept his play.

Let him call you; don't *ever* call him. Why would you put yourself in a position to feel rejected if he does not call back? Besides, if he has to call you, he will hang on to your every word when he does reach you on the phone. Today's girls lose to guys because they are not playing their proper position on the field.

> **"** If he tiptoes out of bounds, walk off the field until he can play fair. **"**

Rule #6—Don't let him kiss you until you know his character, his friends, his family, his intentions and his moves on the field.

There is something so irresistible to a guy when a girl refuses to give in. I did not kiss my husband until he proposed to me, and it was the most romantic kiss I've ever experienced. I was the winner at the game of love. I won the prize ring—and it was worth the wait! Why should you waste your lips on a loser? I'm not saying don't kiss until you're engaged, but do your homework. Wait for a winner.

Rule #7—Don't let him travel "out of bounds."

Imagine yourself wearing a modest pair of shorts and a tank top. Every body part covered is "out of bounds." Once again, tell him honestly what your rules of play are so you both know if they're being broken. If, in the middle of the game, he tiptoes out of bounds, walk off the field until he can play fair. If he tries to break the rules a second time, it's reasonably certain that he's *never* going to play fair, and it's time for you to tell your guy that he needs to find a new team to play on, or to get an accountability coach.

Review the C.H.E.E.R.s Before You Choose Your Team

Give Me a C.H.E.E.R. for the "Safe Sex" team

C—Check out the Impurity Zone.

H—Hand over your heart.

E—Expect to lose respect.

E—Expect pain when you play.

R—Rules were made to be broken.

Let's hear the C.H.E.E.R. for the "Pure Play" team

C—Check out the Pure Power
   Zone.

H—Hold on to your heart.

E—Expect the best.

E—Experience the game in control.

R—Rules are the way to win.

You make the choice; no one can do it for you. A word of caution: Pretending to play on the Pure Play team when your heart belongs to the immoral Safe Sex team *does not* win the game. Be a real player. Don't sit in the middle of the football field where you are an injury waiting to happen. Pick up the ball, and run in the right direction.

Final Coaching Tips

Hopefully by now you've chosen to play on the Pure Play team. Here are some final, winning team tips to keep you tight with your team.

Tip #1—Surround yourself with strong teammates.

You'll never stay strong in your game of purity if you party with the players from the Safe Sex team. I know you are on the field with both teams, but you need to stay on your side of the field. When a ball is thrown to you, hold on tight to your morals, and run in the winning direction. Look for a teammate who will cheer you on, one who will run the same plays you do. Remember that we become whom we surround ourselves with. So be cautious when you pick your friends. You can be nice to the opposing team without being naughty with them.

Tip #2—Study your game.

If you don't like the way the boy players treat you, it's time to study how you play the game. For example, I loved to flirt and have fun with the boys, but I also liked having these boys as "just friends." Because I played the flirting game, I lost the friendship game until a good girlfriend grabbed me by the face mask and said, "Stop playing around with the minds of men just to get attention!" I hated her hard words, but they hit me in a way that changed the way I played my game. I started to learn to play it safe, and boys started to treat me like a winner.

Flirting is not the only wrong play that can get you in trouble. Some of us play "hard ball." We act like we're so tough, but we get mad at the boys when they play rough with us. We treat them unkindly, yet complain they are not sensitive and kind with their words and actions to us.

Letting a boy run over you with his words is another bad play. Learn now to stop the cruel play with some truthful blocking, or he will continue to crush you with tough, tactless words.

The best way to study your own play is to ask one of your fans (your mom, brother or sister, best friend) to watch you in action. If you are going to pass the test with an A+ grade, you have to be willing to let someone quiz you about your action plays with boys.

Tip #3—Be too busy for the boys.

Don't just sit on the bench and wait for some boy to pick you to play. Chances are you will ruin your game with the wrong guy that way. Be the girl who's busy doing activities, homework, family fun, girlfriend things, volunteering somewhere, sports, art and so on. Fill your schedule with fun, faith and fulfilling things that matter. Busy is better than being available for the bad boys just because you are bored. You are also more likely to meet a boy who loves to do the same things, which is a three-point Field Goal!

Tip #4—Create a "Mr. Right" checklist.

Don't let a crush cancel out your checklist. Sometimes we get hit hard in the heart by a boy who knows all the right moves, says all the right things and, of course, is cute to the max. But are his motives in line with your checklist? Is he truly Mr. Right?

The "Mr. Right" *checklist*

❑ Does he bring out the best in you?

❑ Does he treat you like a princess (opens doors, talks with

respect and honor to you and about you)?

❑ Does he pay for all dates?

❑ Does he make you feel important and valued?

❑ Does he honor your rules?

❑ Does he honor your parents' rules?

❑ Does he treat your parents with kindness?

❑ Does he have career and/or college goals?

❑ Does he have a clean mouth, even around his friends?

❑ Does he make you laugh?

❑ Do you feel happy when you are with him?

❑ Does he listen to you without interrupting or "tuning you out"?

❑ Does he remember that what you say matters to you?

I know this is a long list, but you are a girl who deserves the best. Don't waste your playing time on a player who uses his looks, loves with his words only and acts like a loser.

INSTANT Replay

It's never too late to change teams. Today can be a new starting position on the Pure Play team. Don't look back at the bad plays. Learn from them, and then leave them behind you. It's time to be a girl who is a winner, one who gets to pick a "Super

Bowl Boy." You are a "Super Bowl Girl" and a Pure Power Princess, so suit up for the game and play like a star!

"It's never too late to change teams."

YOU GO, GIRL!

Do whatever it takes to stay on the Pure Power team. It's worth the work, and it's worth the wait to win it all! Go for the Super Bowl ring—you deserve it!

GOD TALKS
Sex

God Is...the Creator of Sex

Sometimes it's hard for me to accept the words *sex* and *God* in the same sentence. But God created man and woman, and He created the ultimate expression of their love for one another—sex. So don't let the messed-up media messages about sex stop you from understanding God's plan.

As you already know, I did not know about God or become a Christian until I was twenty-four years old, and I did not understand His plan for purity. I thought there was no way back to purity if you had already played the sex game. But while sitting in a small church during a Good Friday service, I heard a pastor say lovingly, "If any of you are holding on to a secret sin, you are stopping God from making you white as snow." This truth hit my heart, and I wanted to give my last secret sin to God that evening. But I was so ashamed of that secret—my abortion—that I had never confessed it to God for fear of His total disappointment.

God literally used a pastor to help me carry this burden to the cross. The church had set up a big wooden cross in the sanctuary. Each member in the congregation had been handed some paper and nails. The pastor gave us the opportunity to take any hidden sin to the cross and physically nail it there to be left forever.

That Friday I felt God's hand wipe away the last tear about the baby I had aborted. I know I will never feel good about my choice, but I can use the pain to serve as a warning to help those thinking about abortion. I can accept God's forgiveness and move on with my life. I look forward to holding that baby some- day in heaven. If you want to be pure again, pray this prayer with me now.

Dear God, I confess I have sinned sexually, and I'm sorry. I want Your plan for purity today. Please make me pure again in my mind, body and spirit, I pray in Jesus' name. Amen.

For this reason a man will leave his father and his mother and be united to his wife, and they will become one flesh.

—GENESIS 2:24

Are you a
DREAM daughter or a
naughty *nightmare*?

Chapter Five

Parent Talk

Are you feeling brave? I'd like to take you somewhere you'd least expect. It's a place where you hear haunting sounds and see surprisingly scary images. There are plenty of cobwebs and dark corners here, so keep your eyes and ears tuned in...we're going to walk together through a haunted house.

OK, so I don't see you shivering. But even though I steer clear of haunted houses, this one is well worth seeing. So clear your throat, turn the doorknob and let's enter ever so slowly.

Familiar Dark Hallways

Now that we're in the house, you may be wondering why the dark hallway we're standing in feels so familiar. You guessed it—this haunted house is your own house. This is the same hallway where you learned to walk when you were a baby. Now together let's walk down the hall, past the closet (we'll clean out those cobwebs later) and into the living room. Is it truly "living," or is it dead as a doornail? Once this room was very much alive with a friendly little ghost called "you." (OK, you were not a ghost, but I'm desperate to keep with the theme.)

This room is where you learned to love from your parents. When you were afraid, you ran to them for comfort, and in the dark of your fears, their every word gave you confidence. The one thing that frightened you in this house was the thought of being without them.

Now it seems our fears have changed. It's remarkable that our parents, who seemed like such geniuses while we were small children, somehow turned into goons in our minds when we became teens. Now we are afraid to be seen with them. We don't know when it happened, it's just one of those spooky things that happen to teens. Maybe we were abducted by aliens and brainwashed. But who knows?

We used to ask them about everything we wanted to know, and we believed everything they told us. But one spooky morning, we woke up and decided we suddenly knew more than they knew. All at once, those comforting words we loved to hear changed from wonderful to weird.

What, or who, is it that is haunting our homes with subliminal messages that scream, "It's not cool to be close to your parents"? Maybe there are mixed signals coming out of your television or from your friends' actions toward their parents. Could it be that aliens have taken over your TV and zapped the fun right out of your family? Don't expect to get positive principles about good family relationships from much of what you see on television. It seems that some of TV's most creative directors focus on corruption and dysfunction in the home. Maybe their intentions are to comfort those of us who live in scary homes. But that won't bring us close together again.

> **" TV and friends will always be there; your parents won't. "**

Don't misunderstand me—I'm not saying *all* TV shows are haunting our homes. But don't misplace your mind in the middle of much of the trash that can appear. Keep your brain engaged! When your brain goes blank in front of the TV, many messages could capture it and hold your thoughts hostage.

Don't get your mind messed up with life as it's portrayed on TV. It could cause you to act like a monster in your own home and scare your parents with your actions.

You Go, Girl!

Turn off the TV, and turn on the channel in your mind that tunes in to your family. TV and friends will always be there; your parents won't. Don't wait until it's too late.

My dear friend Susan was only twenty years old when her mother died of cancer. She was always close to her mother, but when she hit high school, she pushed her mom away with her words and actions. Sadly she did not see the future. If she had known she only had a few years left with her mom, I'm sure she would have used her mouth for saying "I love you" instead of

> **" Moms and dads need love the most when they deserve it the least. "**

hurting her with her words. Susan's arms would have reached out for one more hug if she had known that there was only a limited supply left. She would have opened her ears to hear her mother's caring words of concern had she known those words were the last she would hear her mother speak. Susan shared with me how hard it was to watch her mom hang on to her last breath. She realized that she had no high school memories of her mother to hang on to.

I'm not trying to scare you about your parents dying. But it's a fact of life that they *are* here for you now. You live with them today. I know parents are not perfect, but neither are daughters. There is a divine reason why your mom and dad were specifically chosen to play the role they have in your life.

I grew up thinking I was in the wrong family because my parents were always fighting, screaming and walking out on each other. When I went over to my friend's home, there was no fighting; in fact, her parents were friendly. Often I wanted to escape from my family or run to the fun, friendly family.

I wasted time tearing my family apart instead of trying to build them up. I was mad at them for fighting and wrecking the fun. Sometimes I thought they would kill each other. But then I would hear them laughing about something "off the wall" in the other room. My dad was a wild and crazy "memory builder."

When my birthday rolled around, he would put billboards up along the California highways telling the world that he loved me.

He brought strange animals to our house from Marineland, things like camels and elephants. I used to be embarrassed by his acts of love, but now I know how lucky I was to be loved by him.

My mom was always trying to plan something spontaneous, but often fights with Dad destroyed her plans. She's not a fighter by nature, so she was locked up inside with pain and fear of the future. I was too young to understand either of these people I called my parents. So I locked them out of my life with my actions and attitude.

I learned that life is hard, and although our families may be freaky, they are still the ones who stay by us regardless of our rudeness and the radical things we do. It may be that some parents are so paralyzed by pain that they pass it on to their children instead of giving God their problems to fix, grabbing on to the power He has to heal them. But we don't have to let their actions keep us in the dark.

My parents divorced when I was thirteen years old. This event rocked *and* relieved my world. They were no longer fighting because they were no longer together. That was a relief. But we were no longer a family because we were apart. That rocked my world.

But over the years I have learned that love conquers all. For many years I spent most of my time haunting my parents with the memories of their mistakes instead of cleaning out my closet, which was filled with cobwebs of unforgiveness. I knew I could not fix their marriage problems, but I wish I had helped to create a happy home instead of adding to the pain and problems.

You can help to make your home a haven, a "safe place." It's not just the parents in the family who do this. We are all in this together. Why not decide to stop scaring your parents with your actions? Go back and light up that dark familiar hallway with love. Moms and dads sometimes need love the most when they deserve it the least. Let's love them today.

Dream or Nightmare quiz

Are you a dream daughter or a naughty nightmare? Do you make your parents happy or horrified? Turn on the light in your dark places with this quiz.

1. You help with the house and pick up your stuff...

   a) Most of the time, trying to do your part to help around the house to take some of the stress off your parents.

   b) Only if you want your parents to do something for you.

2. When there's a warm dinner on the table, you...

   a) Come in, ask how you can help and then wait for everyone to sit before eating. Then you hang out and do the "family thing" for a while.

   b) Sit down and quickly inhale the meal, then exit the family scene ASAP.

3. When you are at home alone with Mom or Dad, you...

   a) Ask them about their day and share the highlights of yours, trying to keep the relationship right.

   b) Ignore them and check into your own world, doing

whatever you want to do regardless of whether they are there or not.

4. When it's your mom's birthday, you...

   a) Make a mushy card for her or buy one that lets her know how much you appreciate her, making sure you're home to celebrate with her on her special day.

   b) May say, "Happy birthday," but you still treat her like she's nothing special.

5. When you want to have a friend over, you...

   a) Talk to your mom about it first to see what works best for her schedule and the rest of the family.

   b) Tell your mom you are bringing someone home without asking if it's OK, because you don't care if it adds stress to her day.

6. Your mom is crying because you hurt her with something you said. You...

   a) Give her a hug and tell her you're sorry and that you love her and feel bad when you hurt her heart.

   b) Get mad at her because she's losing it. Besides, it's her problem if she's in pain. She's a big girl. She can deal with it herself.

7. Your parents agree to let you use their new car until 11:00 P.M. next Friday night, so you...

   a) Thank them for letting you use their new car, clean it up and replace the gas you used. You come home ten minutes early to earn their trust, so you can use it again.

   b) Take advantage of your parents by coming home one hour late, leaving the car a mess and then copping an attitude because they are upset at you.

8. Your friends are waiting for you, and you're totally excited to go out to dinner and a movie. But your parents want you to finish the chores you promised you would do before you leave. You...

   a) Keep your promise and do your chores quickly so you can go. Then you kiss them good-bye and tell them to have a great evening.

   b) Yell at them for expecting you to help around the house and blame them for making your friends wait, then slam the front door without saying good-bye.

9. It's your parent's wedding anniversary, and they want to go on a date night on the same night you made plans without asking them first. You...

   a) Give them a card and make an anniversary cake while they're gone to surprise them when they come home.

   b) Lay a guilt trip on them about wanting to celebrate their marriage and throw a fit if they don't let you go out.

10. Your parents want you to call Grandma or Grandpa to say "hello," so you...

   a) Call, even if you don't feel like it, because you love your parents and grandparents.

   b) Tell them you're too old to call the grandparents and refuse to do what they ask.

11. While you are talking to a friend, your dad mentions that he's expecting a really important phone call. Do you...

   a) Tell your friend that you will call her later and get off the phone immediately with a smile?

   b) Talk back to him in a harsh tone, allowing your friend to hear how "cool" and disrespectful you are to your parents?

12. Your mom has worked hard all day and is feeling exhausted, but she still has to prepare dinner. You... .

   a) Offer to help with dinner and clean up the kitchen while she rests or takes a relaxing bath.

   b) Sit and talk on the phone or watch TV and let her do all the work. Then you complain and whine because you don't like what she cooked and leave the dirty dishes for her to clean after dinner.

13. Your mom offers to take you and a friend on a great vacation. During the vacation, you...

    a) Make sure your mom feels included in your talks and good time. Then you write her a card thanking her for a great time.

    b) Talk back to her in front of your friend, thinking only about what you and your friend want to do, then you forget to thank her for the trip.

14. When your parent comes home from work, you... .

    a) Get up from whatever you are doing to check out what your parent might need, saying "hello" because you care about your parent.

    b) Don't acknowledge your parent is home because you are in your own world. You don't care about your parents unless you need something from them.

15. You borrow a pair of your mom's shoes without asking, and you ruin them in the rain. You...

    a) Tell her you are sorry, and offer to buy her a new pair with your allowance

    b) Throw them back in her closet wet, and don't tell her you wore them.

16. Your mom offers to drive some of the kids on a field trip during the day. You...

   a) Greet her with a hug in front of your friends and ride with her during the trip, then thank her for taking time out of her day to drive you and your friends.

   b) Refuse to ride in her car and pick another mom, totally ignoring her. When she tries to talk to you, you treat her like she's intruding on your time.

Total your A scores _____

Total your B scores _____

10 or more A scores

If your parents are not happy with you with a score like this, then they are the ones in the dark. You are an awesome girl, a delightful daughter, a dream come true for most parents. I'm so impressed with you. Keep lighting up your house with your words, actions and adorable attitude. You go, girl! You're better than having Casper the Friendly Ghost in the house. I don't really believe in ghosts—but I believe you're a blessing to your parents.

5 or more B Scores

Stop scaring your parents with your actions and attitude. Of course your house feels haunted with a scary daughter like you living in it. Clean out the cobwebs in your brain, and resurrect your love for your parents and learn to live with them. Ask yourself one final question: "Do you want a daughter to 'trick or

❝ Even if your parents' words seem weird, listen! Their words could save you from a "monster" experience. ❞

treat' you the way you 'trick or treat' your parents?" It's never too late to change *horrible* to *happy*. You go, girl! Make your parents happy, and you'll live in a happy home again.

Haunted by Your Parents' Weird Words of Wisdom

My dad would be the president of the Parents' Protection Club if there were such a thing. As a teenager, I thought he was a spy for the government or involved with underground crime, because he seemed so paranoid and protective about me.

I was not allowed to leave my house when I was a teen without all the gear. He sent me out totally loaded with a bulletproof vest, rape alarm, Mace spray, beeper, cell phone, flashlight, stun gun and a bunch of weird words of wisdom. OK, I'm exaggerating a little bit, but you know how imprisoned you can feel by your parents' protection.

I used to resent the radical rules for protection until one night when I was out with my girlfriends. Some guys were following us in their car and threatening to kill us. We were flipped out and scared silly. Then I remembered my dad's weird words of wisdom. He said, "If strange guys ever follow you, don't drive home so that they will learn where you live. Call 911, then drive to the nearest police station." So we did, and we were safe. The guys following us were arrested for harassment. My father's weird words of wisdom really worked!

My dad used to talk to me constantly with these weird words of wisdom. He still does. He told me, "If it's dark, never walk out to your car alone. Ask someone to escort you." *What a dork!* I thought.

Then one night I saw a weird-looking, monster man wandering around the mall parking lot. I was scared, and the mall was closing. My dad's weird words of wisdom haunted me once again. I found a security guard to walk me out. Later that night on the news, it was announced that two girls were murdered in that parking lot, right around the same time as when I was leaving.

Even if your parent's words seem weird, listen! Their words could save you from a "monster" experience.

Don't Play "Hide-and-Seek" With Your Parents

When I wanted to go somewhere that my parents did not approve of, I would make up a big story about my plans for the weekend that I knew would sound good to them. Then I would walk out the door and do whatever I wanted to do without letting them know where I really was. I thought I was a good girl by not upsetting them with my real plans. All my friends hid things from their parents to keep peace, so it sounded like the right thing to do—until I got caught.

A friend named Mary wanted to go out of town with her friends for the weekend, and her parents said the big "N-O." She told them she was spending the weekend at my house. Wanting to be a good friend, I covered for her story. All was going well with our "hide-and-seek" plan to keep our parents pleased while doing what we wanted to. On Monday morning, Mary's mom

" Your parents had a warning light implanted in their brain by God on the day you were born. "

showed up at our door to tell us that her daughter had not come home on Sunday. I had no idea where she really was. I was forced to confess that I had been her "cover."

But worse than being caught in a lie was what happened to Mary. She had gone to Reno and was robbed and raped at the campground where she and her friends had gone to drink wine. Her parents drove up to Reno to pick her up from the hospital.

Mary was never the same. But she and I learned not to play the game of "hide-and-seek" with our parents. Hiding the truth just spells *t-r-o-u-b-l-e*. Don't play the hiding game. Seek your parents' approval for your plans, then hide what they say in your heart and do it!

Parents Know When We Are in the Dark

Your parents had a warning light implanted in their brain by God on the day you were born. Somehow, when their children are in trouble, many parents feel the flash going on and off to warn them to help. Whether your parents are in tune with you or not, it's worth paying attention to their warning.

My friends and I were driving to Lake Tahoe when I was twenty-four and were having a great time. All of a sudden I remembered that before I left, my stepmom Susie had told me to pay attention to my feelings when fear hits. Then she prayed for our safety. She said she felt that something might happen to my girlfriends and me as we drove. At the time we were driving, I did not know why that thought had been triggered in my mind, but suddenly something made me grab the steering wheel while my friend was driving and steer us off the road right into a ditch.

My friends were so mad at me for the crazy reaction. But while they were yelling at me, two huge Mac trucks were racing side by side on the two-lane highway on which we had been driving. We soon realized that if I had not jerked us off the road when I did, the trucks would have killed us in a head-on collision. When we realized that God had spared our lives, we hugged each other and cried happy tears of thankfulness.

Later that night when we checked into the hotel, I called my stepmom to tell her what had happened. She asked me what time it took place. I told her it had been 11:00 P.M. She said that right at that time she had been falling asleep, but suddenly she fell out of bed onto the floor and begged God to spare my life and protect my friends and me.

This is just one of many stories I could share that would give you goose bumps all night. Our parents are more aware of when we are in trouble than anyone.

I once read that becoming a parent means you're giving your heart permission to walk outside of your body for the rest of your life. Don't get hit with a big scary surprise. Listen to your parents' warnings, and let them cover you in prayer.

Resurrect Your Dead Attitude

A young girl named Ann disliked everything about her

❝ Something miraculous happens as we invest our hearts and time into making our homes happy. ❞

mother. Every day she would avoid her mother like the plague, trying to think of ways to hurt her for all the things her mom had done and said to hurt her.

One day she was telling her best friend, Barb, about her thoughts, and Barb came up with a great idea for revenge. The plan was for Ann to be the best daughter possible for six weeks. Ann was to do everything her mother said with a smile. She was not to argue and try to win her way. Every day Ann would tell her mother that she loved her. At the end of the six weeks, Ann's final revenge would be to crush her mother's heart by running away. It was the perfect plan!

After six weeks, Barb and Ann got together to plan the "run away." Barb asked Ann if she had all of her belongings packed and ready to go. Finally Ann said, "I can't do it. Somehow, in these past six weeks I've learned to love my mom again. I want to stay home with her."

It's amazing to see how our heart changes when we look for ways to love our family. Something miraculous happens as we invest our hearts and time into making our homes happy.

Leave the Light On

Before we leave the haunted house, let's shine the light on

the things we've seen and heard about our parents and our-selves. Remember that it's cool to be close. Do the family thing—show your love now! Because our families are the foundation of our futures, even if you do not have the perfect mother or father, you can still learn from their mistakes. By doing so, someday you will be able to build your own family foundation through what you learned and through your faith in God.

YOU GO, GIRL!

Be the daughter you want to have someday.

FATHER GOD
Talks

God Is...the Ultimate Father

I have a father who would make the sun shine 24/7 and color the moon pink for me if he could. I can always count on him to do what he says. He is a man of his word and an excellent financial provider for his family. Those of us who have fathers to love us sometimes take that love for granted. The sad truth is that a huge percentage of the girls in America do not have a father they can count on to be there for them.

Regardless of whether or not your earthly father can be counted upon to be there for you, you have our ultimate Father in heaven who is always there to love and listen to you. He is the Comforter and Corrector, and He is completely committed to taking care of us. He loves you so much. If He had a wallet, He would carry your picture in it to show the world how wonderful He thinks you are.

A girl named Ashley called me to tell me that her best friend, Cindy, was dying of AIDS. It was Cindy's final days, and she did not know her heavenly Father. As Ashley began to share with me about Cindy's life, I started to cry uncontrollably. I had never heard a story about abuse that severe. I won't go into the gross details, but I want to confess to you that I was mad at God for not stopping her father and many other men from hurting her so horribly.

To make matters worse, Ashley wanted me to call Cindy at the hospital and tell her about God's love and His plan for paradise before she died. At the time, I told Ashley that I did not think I was the one to share God's love with her because I couldn't relate to her. But I promised to pray for her.

Ashley called me every day for the next five days saying, "Cindy needs you to call. She loves your books, but she hates God for her life. I beg you, please call. She's about to die."

I broke down and called. I'll never forget how I felt as I dialed Cindy's hospital room. My heart was broken for her, my emotions were out of control thinking about her, and my spirit was wrestling with my heavenly Father. But once I heard her voice, God filled my mouth with these words: "Cindy, I know you've been terribly abused by your father. But don't let his actions keep you from going into the arms of a heavenly Father who will never hurt you. He will wipe away every tear you've ever cried here on earth."

Cindy did not say anything, so I began to pray, and then we hung up the phone. After the call I prayed harder than ever for her, begging God to help her to heaven.

One week later I received a phone call from Ashley. "Cindy died this morning," she said, "but last night she told me to tell you that she forgave her father and accepted Jesus. She said she will see you in paradise someday."

Don't let any man's actions keep you from your heavenly Father's love and your eternal home. Many innocent people suffer because of sin. Keep an eternal perspective! Know that someday all abusive people who inflict pain on others on earth will suffer that pain *forever* in a tormented place called *hell*.

I promise you that God is a just God, and He will not let their actions go unpunished.

Dear God, please help me to see the hard things in life through the eyes of eternity. Give me the courage to help hurting people find You.

If you, then, though you are evil, know how to give good gifts to your children, how much more will your Father in heaven give good gifts to those who ask him!

—MATTHEW 7:11

Pumped up
with **PMS**!

Chapter Six

Heart-to-Heart Talk

Are you out of control with P.M.S. and *not* loving it?

You Know You're P.M.S.ing When...

❀ You freak out so badly from breaking one nail that you break the other nine so they will match.

❀ You burst out crying in class and then throw yourself on the floor just because your teacher did not call on you to answer a question.

❀ You shave your head bald just because you are having a bad hair day.

❀ You smash your favorite food in your face because you are pigging out at such high speeds that you don't give your mouth time to open.

❀ You totally lose it in line at the movie theater

because people crowded in line in front of you to get popcorn and soda, causing you to steal their popcorn bucket and run!

OK, this is a little over the edge, but have you ever felt out of control emotionally—like you could not get a grip on your reactions? P.M.S. is not the cause of all your emotional problems; many times when we don't deal with issues, they deal with us.

I grew up in a family that freaked out about everything! One time my dad and I were in line at the grocery store, with a lady and her daughter in line in front of us. The woman was buying her groceries with coupons. My dad became very out of control as he waited for them to count and compare their coupons. Finally he grabbed the coupons out of their hands and ripped them into shreds. Then he yelled at them to get the "blankety-blank" out of his way, and pushing them aside, he paid their bill—and ours. He almost knocked them over trying to get past them to leave the scene of the crime. At least they got free groceries from the Grinch!

My mother was extremely emotional. I spent most of my childhood on the upside-down, inside-out, wild roller-coaster ride of life. It seemed I was always screaming on the inside for someone to turn off the emotional roller coaster.

So what's the deal with how we feel? How do we exit the emotional "out-of-control zone" and enter into the right reaction zone?

Believe it or not, being emotionally out of control is a warning flag from God. Something in our life needs to be dealt with. And keep in mind, you don't have to freak out *loudly* to be out of control. You can be just as out of control inside, and no one will know by the way you look on the outside.

Life isn't perfect.

We all deal with emotional stuff a little differently. Terri Talker may deal with her emotions by pretending her pain is not real, by eating out of control or chang-ing the channel to something fun or distracting. Debbie Doer might say, "I can handle hurt. Nothing bothers me." Or Debbie Doer might be out of control with a schedule so jam-packed that she doesn't allow herself to heal. Thelma Thinker may get lost in her book or become very critical of herself and others. Pamela Peacemaker might hide her hurts and dive into everyone else's pain to avoid dealing with her own. Regardless of how we deal with our issues or show it, we all have emotional stuff.

Out of control is not just an outward display of insanity. If we don't deal with how we feel, it will deal with us. Many of us are moody but don't know why. Others are weepy without reason or angry about everything but can't pinpoint the cause of the anger. Fear can freak us out, and sometimes a small disappointment devastates us. Our insecurities interrupt our inner peace.

How can we stop the emotional roller coaster and enjoy the ride of reality? First we have to get a grip on why God gave us the feelings in the first place. I mean, why can't we just feel happy?

Because *life isn't perfect.* We are not perfect, which means we are all going to get hurt or hurt someone else at times. But all of us have the ability to handle our hearts when hurt harasses us with an onslaught of bad emotions.

How well do you handle your heart? Take this quiz to find out how well you do in life's harassing moments:

Heart-to-Heart *quiz*

1. When you are feeling angry with someone, you...

    A. Tell the person about your anger, and you work it out.

    B. Hold a grudge because you don't want to deal with it.

    C. Make it your mission to get even. You never forgive that person because they don't deserve forgiveness.

2. When you feel fear or freak out about something, you...

    A. Pray and then trust God to free you from fear.

    B. Think about your fear all the time, but you don't let it paralyze you from living life.

    C. You can't do anything but freeze up and drive yourself crazy.

3. You have a bad attitude...

    A. Rarely.

    B. Sometimes.

    C. Most of the time.

4. You are bummed out...

    A. Rarely.

    B. Sometimes.

    C. Most of the time.

5. You feel tired and unmotivated about doing anything...

   A. Rarely.

   B. Sometimes.

   C. Most of the time.

6. Do you take everyone's stress and problems personally?

   A. Rarely.

   B. Sometimes.

   C. Most of the time.

7. When you feel out of control emotionally, you...

   A. Pray and ask God to help you do the right thing.

   B. Handle it in any way you feel like handling it at the moment, although you somewhat hold yourself "in check."

   C. Scream, throw a temper tantrum or do something really stupid that you regret later.

Scoring Your Answers

Write down the total points in each category below:

Total all your A scores   _____

Total all your B scores   _____

Total all your C scores   _____

A scores—3–7 total points

It seems like you've learned to deal with your emotions

openly and honestly. In other words, no deep hurts are hidden in your heart. Keep being real!

B scores—3–7 total points

OK, on the outside it may look like life is going good, but let's go to the next level and turn your heart toward greatness.

C scores—3–7 total points

You need more than a "chill pill." You need some stress relief and a plan of action for your reactions. But don't worry; it will happen as you get on your way to the right reaction zone and begin to exit out of the "losing-it life."

So What's the Deal With How We Feel?

I'm sure that at times you feel as though you are a mishmash of both bad and good emotions. I've discovered that emotions are the music of life. For example, think about your favorite movie. Can you imagine watching that movie without any music track? NOT!

We girls love music so much that it actually affects how we feel about the movie! We may even run right out to buy the movie soundtrack so we can relive that emotional movie experience again and again.

The soundtrack to our movie of life has the same effect on us, good or bad. Emotions touch our hearts. So don't try to disconnect the cable to your feelings. Instead, let's learn how to deal with our feelings so we can be free from a life on "pause." A great day is a terrible thing to waste!

You Go, Girl!

Listen to the warnings that alert you to the presence of negative emotions (fear, anger, jealousy, depression, worry, exhaustion, lack of energy for life). Respond by using P.M.S.:

Plan of Action for Our Reactions

P—Pray.

Don't play at being your own god. Let God have your heart. Pray immediately when negative emotions surface. Then, on a piece of paper, write down what your feelings are and how those emotions made you feel and act. I've learned not to do anything until I've calmed down inside.

M—Make a plan.

Seek out advice from someone you trust who is older and wiser than you. Make sure that person loves you—and loves God and knows the Bible. Don't take free advice from the wrong person. It could cost you a big price and become a mistake you'll regret. Then once you have received good advice, write out your plan, and do it.

S—Set your mind to deal with the feelings.

It's a choice you make. Deal with negative emotions the excellent way—God's way as listed above. Get in the right reaction zone. When you feel like letting negative emotions take con-

 **"A great day is a terrible thing to waste!"**

trol of your mind and heart, choose to follow your plan, and you'll love life. You will have done the right thing, and you will have no regret.

Deactivating Disappointment

No matter how old you are, you've lived long enough to know that life does not always work out the way you want it to work out. I've learned that disappointment is sometimes merely a detour to something greater. God closes some doors in our lives, and it's important that we remember to get our faces out of His way so the closing door doesn't hurt so much.

Jennie, a friend of mine, loved her grandfather more than anything, but she did not get to see him very often. When he came to visit she wanted to go everywhere with him. One afternoon he took off without her for the day. She was very disappointed. It devastated her because it was the last day of his visit.

Later that evening, her family received a very painful phone call. A drunk driver had killed her grandfather and everyone in the car with him. Although Jennie had been so disappointed that she couldn't go with her grandfather, her disappointment was the detour that saved her young life.

Disappointment also has a way of teaching us something about ourselves. When I directed the Miss Teen Arizona Pageant, during the week of rehearsals all the girls had great attitudes. They were awesome, but I knew that once the judges picked the winner, many of those girls would change from Cinderella to the wicked stepsister in their hearts. So before the final pageant night, I lovingly reminded each girl that if her attitude changed after the new Miss Teen Arizona was picked, then the judges must have picked the right girl. Disappointment is our opportunity to put our true character to the test.

YOU GO, GIRL!

To deactivate disappointment, we must react with **P.M.S.**

- ❀ ***Pray for our attitude.*** When disappointment hits, it's hard to handle it by ourselves. Sometimes we need a supernatural heart makeover. God is the heart healer and makeover expert. Call on Him.

- ❀ ***Make a choice to react the right way.*** Wait until you pray and calm down before reacting. Then when you are ready, do the right thing.

- ❀ ***Stop and think about what we can learn from the experience.*** Write down your disappointment and what brought healing. Then write down what you learned through the experience.

❀ Girl POWER Prayer ❀

Dear God, give me the ability to learn to trust Your detours even when I feel disappointed.

❝ We don't have to hand the power over to people, friends or family to make or break our day. ❞

Intercepting Insults

Let's talk football again! Even if you're not into the game, you can't help but hear the crowds cheer when someone intercepts a football in the middle of a play and begins running toward the opposite goalpost. That's what we're going to learn to do in the Gabby Game of Insults. We're going to stop the ball of fire from someone's tongue and win the mind game over that person's insensitive insults.

We don't have to hand the power over to people, friends or family to make or break our day. Remember, people who hurt, hurt other people. So before you receive a ball of insults from anyone, look at who's throwing that ball. If that person is not playing ball by using the "winner's playbook," don't receive what they say. Always consider the source before you allow anyone to ruin your game of confidence.

I grew up around a lot of negative people. Many times we become what we surround ourselves with, so I began to become what people said about me. Kids can be cruel when you are not "Miss Popular." I did not know how to intercept their insults when I was young. Today I've learned the intercept rules well. So if you are tired of being hit in the heart, pay attention to the rules I'm about to teach you, and you will win every time.

Rule #1—Don't allow someone's words or actions to

stop you from winning what you want out of life.

I was a people-pleasing approval addict, so I could be wiped out with hurtful words easily. I had an English teacher who, in front of the class, told me that I was born to lose. My mother always pointed out how much better my friends were than me. My friends never encouraged me, because they were just as messed up as I was. But something happened when I decided I was going to be a winner over their words. I didn't look to them for approval anymore. I looked to God for my confidence, and that made me strong enough to handle the hurtful tackles of their tongue.

Rule #2—Don't play by another's dirty rules.

Whenever you get into a mud fight, everyone gets messed up and dirty. When someone insults me, I've learned to trust God to be my defense. In other words, stop talking, and eventually the insults will be intercepted by your silence.

When someone says to me, "I heard...blah blah..." (something bad about me), rather than defending myself and getting mad, I consider the source. I look at the person who is passing on the ugly rumor, and I say, "I'm sorry you chose to believe that about me." Saying this intercepts the insult and returns the power to win back to you.

Rule #3—Pray for the person who insults you.

I know it sounds crazy to do nothing but pray, but it's not. If you pray a blessing on the person causing you pain, you give your heart a way of escaping from those hurtful words. But if you don't pray for them, you will begin to hate and hurt, and that combination will not win the mind game over your emotions.

You Go, Girl!

Rules Recap:
>**P**ass on receiving their insults.
>**M**ake up your mind to win despite them.
>**S**tart praying for the person right away.

✿ Girl POWER Prayer ✿

Dear God, let me see myself through Your eyes so what others say won't affect how I feel.

Facing Fear

Believe it or not, fear can be the very thing that saves us...

❀ ***Fear of going to jail*** can keep us from breaking the law.

❀ ***Fear of getting pregnant or catching AIDS*** can keep us sexually pure.

❀ ***Fear of the future*** can cause us to stay close to God.

❀ ***Fear of failing*** can be used as a motivator to make us do our best.

❀ ***Fear of danger*** can save our lives.

❀ ***Fear of consequences for our actions*** can keep us on the right road.

But there is a fear that can freeze you up inside or cause you to do something foolish. When I was in high school, I lived in constant fear of rejec-

66 Face fear head-on. 99

tion. I could not handle the thought that someone somewhere on my campus might not want to be my friend. This fear turned me into a people-pleasing approval addict.

One time I was hanging out in front of a grocery store with some friends when they challenged me to go into the store and steal some candy. Some of them had already stolen some soda and cigarettes. Because I feared losing their friendship more than I feared being arrested for shoplifting candy, I went into the store. While I was waiting in line to buy some chips, I grabbed several candy bars.

As I left quickly, expecting to receive the applause of my friends for my performance, I was met by two police officers—with handcuffs—who hauled me off to juvenile hall (jail for kids). As I rode in the back of that police car, all I could think about was how I had let fear force me to do something so stupid. I was not even the type of girl who likes to steal. Thankfully my dad came to get me, and they dropped the "candy crime" charges.

Fear can cause us to react to things that will never happen. For example: Fear of losing a friend might make you act jealous and controlling toward that person. Fear of being fat has turned more than eight million girls bulimic. Fear of not being loved by a boy causes many girls to sleep with their boyfriends. The list of self-destruction caused by fear is endless.

Face fear head-on. Maybe your fear is not as severe as the

things I've listed above, but if fear disrupts your day and consumes your thoughts, it needs to be faced with P.M.S.

You Go, Girl!

Pray—turn your fear into faith. Tell yourself, "He is God, I am not!"

Make the choice not to react out of fear.

Set boundaries on what you will and will not do. Write down your boundaries. Then when fear hits, you will remember your boundaries.

A final word about fear: Fear and worry are the darkroom where negatives are developed.

Girl POWER Prayer

Dear God, help me to face all my fear with faith in You.
Let positive fear keep me protected from doing things I will
regret later in life.

Dealing With Depression

What is depression? It's a hopeless, exhausted, I'm-not-

having-fun, life-stinks, get-out-of-my-face, I-can't-deal-with-it, leave-me-alone, let-me-eat-chocolate state of mind. That just about sums it up.

Depression is attacking girls and women all over the world. Believe it or not, the top-selling drug in our country is a drug for depression. If you have some depressed days, don't get paranoid on me—we all have them. But when days turn into weeks, and weeks turn into months, it's time to deal with depression. And you should know how to deal with depression, how to break free of a cycle of bad days.

It's easy to fall into the deep pit of depression. There are so many negative forces that hit us in the heart. So let's deal with it and dump the junk that holds us hostage to a hopeless heart.

THE F.R.E.E.D.O.M. {P L A N}

F—Face the fact you need to do something about the depressed place you're in. Don't deny it. Don't ignore it. Don't decorate it. Deal with it, so it will stop dealing with you.

R—Run to God with your hopeless heart. When I deal with depression, I cry out to God. I mean I actually tell Him that I hate life right at that moment. I tell Him that I have no hope or reason to go on, so I need Him to roll the stone away from my hard heart and give me back my purpose, power and peace—NOW!

E—Energize your life! The best way to get up and get out of depression is to fast (give up) all white sugar, white flour and

dairy products. In other words, stop using the "white stuff." These foods can cause exhaustion and confusion in our minds, and they are proven to cause depression. One study completed at a mental hospital took all patients off white sugar and white flour. Within six weeks, 80 percent of their mental health was restored, and they were free to go. If you want further research on sugar, buy the best-selling book *Sugar Blues* by William Dufty.[1] What the white stuff does to our minds, bodies and emotions will blow you away.

Caution: Don't turn fake. The blue and pink packets (artificial, sugar-free) are even worse. Fast from fake, and fast from white, and after a few days with a detox headache, which goes away, you will see a whole new world. You will love the way you see it!

E—Exercise! There is no greater antidepressant than sucking air. Exercise releases endorphins into your bloodstream. Endorphins make you happy. Exercise gives oxygen to your brain so you can think clean. Even if you don't feel like it, "Just do it!" Nike gives good advice!

Don't just sit around depressed. Get up; move your body, and dump the junk. You will be amazed at how it will change your state of mind. Thirty minutes of sucking air is worth more than any vitamin, any TV show and any good book. We're talking about your life and your ability to handle it.

D—Deal with the root of the depression. Many things cause weeds to grow in our garden of life, and weeds kill our beautiful garden. Write down all the things that cause you to be depressed, and then deal with them, one at a time. When I lost all my weight, dropped sugar from my diet and started exercising, my depression went away for a long time. However, it returned a few years later.

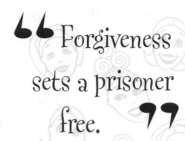

66 Forgiveness sets a prisoner free. 99

I did not understand that although I was eating healthy, exercising, praying, reading my Bible and going to church I still had weeds growing in my garden. One weed was *unforgiveness*. I still did not forgive my mom for hurting me with her words or my dad for his temper or both of them for getting a divorce. These three weeds in my garden were working against all my efforts to be the best version of me. So I wrote letters to both of my parents, telling them I loved them. Then I set some boundaries so I would no longer let them use words to hurt me. Once I did this, the weeds died, and the roots of my depression were ripped out.

If someone has badly wounded you, you will be held captive to that hurt until you offer forgiveness to that individual. Forgiveness sets a prisoner free. Once you forgive, you will realize that the prisoner was you.

O—Offer help to someone today. You will be amazed at how helping someone else will give you a vacation from your own problems. Be refreshed. My refreshing did not come until I started to pray for God to show me ways to encourage or help someone else.

Every day that I experience total freedom from a "down in the dumps" day, life really takes on new meaning. I finally realized that there are more important things in life than me and my

problems. I call it the "get-out-and-get-over-it" solution. God has a purpose for pain—and that purpose is to enable you to help someone else through the same experiences from which you came. Paul advises us, "He [God] comforts us when we are in trouble, so that we can share that same comfort with others in trouble" (2 Cor. 1:4, CEV). So take a moment right now, and pray your way to make someone else's day.

M—Move on. Once you've cried out to God, ripped the root of depression out, fasted off the white stuff, started exercising and prayed to make someone's day—move on! Don't look back. Forget the past. It is not your future.

I not longer dwell on the fact that I did not come from the perfect family… that I made a bunch of bad mistakes… that my English teacher said I'm a loser… and on and on and on. If I did, I would not be writing this book, speaking at conferences or loving my husband and children. I would probably gain all sixty pounds back and start using drugs again.

The day came when I really knew who I was—who God created me to be—and that what happened to me in the past is long gone. This is a new day… not a perfect day, but a new day. Even though I still make mistakes, just like everyone else, mistakes are the very things that make us wise. Pain makes us passionate for others. So what if you blow it? Repent to God, make it right, turn and move on to your new life!

You Go, Girl!

Deal with depression with P.M.S.

Pray for peace, power and purpose.

Move your body with exercise.

Stop eating and drinking the white artificial stuff.

✿✿ Girl POWER Prayer ✿✿

Dear God, turn my pain into power and purpose to help others.

The Music of Your Heart

Don't fall in love with "sucker songs"—music that causes you to think about sex, suicide and sad things in life. Music can be the magic that motivates you to excellence, or it can be the very thing that seduces your soul into being the sucker that drowns your dreams. Guard your heart. It's the power of who you are and what you are becoming.

I did not realize how powerful the music I loved was until I attended a rock concert with my friends where a riot broke out in the audience as the musicians sang a song about war. That night, some of the kids hearing that music killed themselves.

Write out or read the words—without the music—of your favorite songs. If the words send messages that you don't agree with, don't listen any longer. You're too awesome to be brain-washed into becoming a bad girl. Never let your heart guard go on vacation. Keep it with you at all times. You need it to protect your heart.

Don't play mind games with your heart.

" *You will never regret guarding your greatest power— your power to think smart.* **"**

You don't have to put on a blindfold to guard your mind. All you have to do is to dump the junk that makes your head swim with confusion and causes your dreams to die. What we read will control what we think. Why should we let ugly fish swim in our private pools? I don't know about you, but I love to swim in clean waters that are crystal clear. To win the final category of the Girl Power Game, you will need your mind.

When I was involved in beauty pageants, all I read was beauty magazines. Eventually these beauty magazines and their articles about beauty and boys consumed my mind. All I ever thought about was my body and my beauty. Sadly, my mind's obsession with body and beauty made me a bulimic for many years. Today I don't waste my time reading anything that wastes my mind. You will never regret guarding your greatest power— your power to think smart. So lifeguard your heart!

Watch, read and listen only to excellence. Invest your time toward winning your goals. No more compromising. You have too much to lose to pollute your clear, clean mind.

YOU GO, GIRL!

Lifeguard your heart with P.M.S.

Pray for protection and wisdom.

Make a choice about what you read, watch or listen to.

Set a new standard of excellence.

❀ Girl POWER Prayer ❀

Dear God, give me the supernatural ability to hear and see what I'm doing to my mind, body and soul.

HEART-TO-HEART
Review

❀ Deactivate disappointment with P.M.S.

Pray about your disappointment, and let God change your attitude.

Make the choice to react in a way you won't regret.

Stop and think what you can learn from it.

❀ Intercept insults with P.M.S.

Pass on receiving the insult, consider the source and remember that hurting people hurt people.

Make up your mind to win despite their words.

Start praying for the person right away.

❀ Face fear with P.M.S.

    Pray to turn fear into faith.

    Make the choice not to react out of fear.

    Set boundaries of what you will let fear do to you.

❀ Deal with depression with P.M.S.

    Pray for peace, power and purpose.

    Move your body with exercise.

    Stop eating and drinking "the white stuff."

❀ Lifeguard your heart with P.M.S.

    Pray for protection and wisdom.

    Make a choice about what you read, watch or listen to.

    Set a new standard of excellence.

I pray that by this time the acronym P.M.S. has taken on a whole new meaning for you. Now that you've read this chapter, you have the tools to use to keep your heart healthy, holy and happy. You've learned to handle your heart with your head and prayer. So let's get a grip, and get a life without fear, depression, disappointment or confusion.

GOD TALKS
Healing

God Is...the Heart Specialist

God is the heart specialist. He does more than listen to our hearts; He diagnoses the cause of the pain or problem supernaturally. He removes it surgically without leaving any scars.

People often ask me, "How can you talk about your past without crying or resurrecting all the pain again and again?"

My answer is, "My past is there to teach me, not torment me." I faithfully took God's advice and medicine for my soul by forgiving people and reading His Word. He removed the very roots of guilt, regret and unforgiveness. Truly I am free from who I was and on fire about my new life in Christ.

However, after my spiritual and emotional *heart surgery* with God, it took time, tears and some strong ministry medicine for the total healing to happen.

His Word says in Isaiah 43:2, "When you cross deep rivers, I will be with you, and you won't drown. When you walk through fire, you won't be burned or scorched by the flames" (CEV).

He is the heart doctor who never leaves you. He is on call at all times to heal your hurts and carry your concerns. He is waiting now and forever to hear from you. I've seen and heard a lot of people's pain in my ten years of touring and talking. Sometimes it's overwhelming to me because I want to make it better personally with my words. When there is a serious illness in someone's heart, I'm not a specialist. But God is!

I immediately take each person to the Heart Doctor in prayer.

Then I direct them to a Christian counselor or pastor to help with the healing process. I've seen many miracles and major heart changes. But I've also seen people try to heal themselves in their own way, and it never lasts. The heart sickness always returns, and when it does it is even worse.

I became acquainted with a young girl whose mother did not love her. She had been abused emotionally since she was just a little girl. I cried with her, prayed with her and even became somewhat of a spiritual mother to her. But she could not stop the hurt.

One day I said to her, "I want you to volunteer in the church nursery with the toddlers. I want you to love those kids the way you wish you had been loved as a child." So she did. After one year with the kids, God had totally healed her heart. She decided to go to college and get her degree in childcare management. Today she is free from that heart pain. She heads up a preschool.

Sometimes healing takes place when we become to others the very thing we never had in our own life. Whatever the case, God wants us to hand over all the pieces so He can glue our hearts back together by using His special supply of restoration and healing.

Dear God, I don't want to be my own doctor. I want to call on You when I'm in pain. Please help me to remember that You are always on call for me, and for my friends and family.

On hearing this, Jesus said, "It is not the healthy who need a doctor, but the sick."
—MATTHEW 9:12

Get your passport to
PARADISE.

Chapter Seven

God Talk

We're at the end of our GirlTalk time together, and I've had such a blast babbling to you. Thanks! I hope you had a good time while we giggled, grew and got into some personal stuff together. The last talk I want to have with you is about a place called *Paradise*. It's the ultimate Spring Break Vacation where the fun in the *Son* never ends.

The Never-Ending Vacation

Have you ever gone somewhere that you did not want to leave because you were having such a good time? Life seemed wonderful while you were there. I have done that. My dad started an advertising agency when I was a teenager, and his specialty was working with beautiful, five-star resort hotels in amazing places. Because these hotels were his accounts, he was given a big budget for free vacations.

❝The President of Paradise is God Himself.❞

And I'm not just talking free rooms—I'm talking free food, free recreation, full use of the spa, tennis, golf, swimming pool and, of course, maid service and room service.

Every spring break I would invite my girlfriends on a paradise vacation totally paid for by my dad. Remember, I was a "party girl" in high school. But I was also still dealing with a lot of pressures from my parent's divorce, pain from my past choices and, of course, "life." So these get-aways were great vacations from my problems.

I loved checking out of the daily hassles and into a hotel that had everything I needed to hang out and have fun in the sun. I felt at home in these hotels and resorts. One time while my friends and I were lying on the beach on a perfect sunny day, with cute waiters bringing us food, drinks and towels, I said to my friends, "This is my life. Why can't I live it forever? If I had it my way, I would check into the Presidential Suite of a five-star resort by the water and live on a Paradise vacation until I die."

I had no idea at the time that there really was a place like Paradise where I could live forever, a place where I could have a permanent vacation from the pressures of life. In this Paradise we can hang out together by a sea that is so brilliant and beautiful that it appears to have real crystals floating on the water, with light reflecting so amazingly that it warms your heart. It is a place so peaceful that there no one is stressed out, bummed out or burned out. It is a place so safe there is no crime, so heart-warming and happy that it soothes your soul.

This Paradise is a place so out of this world that it's impossible to describe. The President of Paradise is God Himself, the Creator of the universe.

God has sent each of us a passport, His Son, that allows us to check in forever at the Heavenly Hotel. There are more dreamy details you can discover there. Real angels fly through the air, which is filled with music so magical that it's like your favorite song times infinity. When you check into the Heavenly Hotel, you get an incredible free gift from God—you get to exchange your body for a perfect body. And check this out— your perfect body never gets sick and will never die.

Last but not least, love is always in the air. No one can ever hurt you in any way, because people who cause pain can only get a passport to cross the border if they ask God's forgiveness and change the way they live on earth. This eternal spring break-away place is radiant with God's never-ending light and love shining on your precious face.

It sounds too good to be true, doesn't it? Believe it or not, this heavenly place is a virtual reality you can experience forever, if you have the passport to get in.

If you will allow me to do so, I want to act as your travel agent. Let me help you to reserve a room at the Heavenly Hotel (compliments of my Father in heaven).

Let's Talk Eternity

Eternity is something I never thought about when I was in high school. But one day a drug dealer from whom I used to buy drugs when I was a party girl went to a Christian camp over the weekend. He came back to school totally different in every way. His hard heart began to turn into a caring heart. His foul mouth, once filled with curses, was now filled with a message about heaven. Instead of information about the weekend parties, he gave me information about how to receive the real high found in Jesus.

I did not want to hear his message, but I could not help but notice his life on campus. I had no idea how much this ex-druggie was going to be used as my travel agent to get me a passport to Paradise. Every time this boy passed me in the hall, he would say, "I'm praying for you, Sheri Rose." I never took him seriously, but I was not going to pass on his prayers.

Eight years later I checked into a hotel room with the intention of checking out of life permanently. I could not break free from my bulimia and bad choices, and I was out of "more-about-me" ideas to make me happy. As I stood there in the hotel bathroom, hopelessly holding a bottle full of sleeping pills, I screamed at God, "If You are real, then help me!" I did not take those pills that night. I just cried myself to sleep. In a dream I saw that drug dealer's kind face and loving eyes, and I heard him say, "I'm praying for you. God has a place for you in Paradise, and Jesus is the way to get there."

The next morning when I woke up, I wanted to know more about Paradise and about Jesus, so once again I asked God to show me a glimpse of heaven if it was reality. He did. My boyfriend invited me to his grandparent's house for dinner, and there I saw a glimpse of heaven. I saw two people who were still in love after fifty years of marriage. I saw peace and purpose in their lives, and in their actions I felt love that doesn't cost any-thing.

I want these people to be my own family, I thought as I visited with them. Just as I had that thought, Emily, the seventy-year-old grandma, said, "Sheri Rose, would you like to check out of your hotel while you're here and check into our house?"

I didn't take even take a second to think about it. Excitedly I said a big, "YES!" Then I asked them, "Do you know if heaven is a real place?" I asked the right

" "God sent His only Son to pay your entry fee into heaven." "

people the right questions. They were Christian missionaries.

They spent every night taking me through the Bible Brochure to give me directions on how to get my passport. I hung on to every word, which is a miracle in itself because I never stop talking long enough to hang on to anyone's word.

I had everything I wanted, but I still felt insecure, empty and tired of trying to position myself for "the perfect life." I'm one of those girls who want it all. But even after I got it all—boyfriends, money, success, beauty titles, modeling contracts—I wanted to exchange it all for something better, because it was not worth the price I had to pay to keep it.

I still remember sitting in front of the fire and sipping tea with my boyfriend's grandmother, Emily. Suddenly she asked me, "What is your heart's deepest desire?"

"To be Miss USA this year," I shot back instantly. Lovingly she told me about the greatest crown of all—the Crown of Life, appointed by God Himself. This crown represented what I had been searching for all my life, the purpose and power to do great things.

"How can I win the crown?" I asked.

> **The more I get to know God, the more He gives.**

She replied, "Someone already won it for you. God sent His only Son to pay your entry fee into heaven. He wants to place an eternal crown that never breaks or fades on your head."

I wanted the crown, but this Jesus thing sounded too good to be true. How could it be that a King would die on a cross so I could win a new life? I had worked so hard up to that point on my new look, my new career, my new body and my new friends that the thought of winning something without working for it was beyond my comprehension.

Emily never pushed me to say what I call the "Passport Prayer" to heaven, but she did leave me directions on how to get there. Two months later, in another hotel room by myself with sleeping pills in hand, I cried out to God. I asked His Son, Jesus, to give me freedom from bulimia and depression and to give me a new life here in earth.

He gave me all I asked for—and more. He gave me new eyes to see the world with a new perspective and a heart for *people* instead of *things*. He made a way for me to do what I loved to do—talk and travel. But He didn't stop there. Once I was ready to win people for Paradise, He even let me win the Mrs. United States title. But the crown appointed by the panel of judges is nothing compared to the crown of life appointed by God.

The more I get to know God, the more He gives. He gave me a loving husband even though I did not feel I deserved it. He gave me two healthy beautiful babies even though I had an abortion. He helped me to love my parents again regardless of their actions, and now we have a close relationship. He turned my pain into purpose. He gave me my dream family with my in-laws. I'm not saying life is always perfect now that I am a Christian, but life always has purpose, and I have the power in God to persevere when the pressure is on!

Leave Directions to Paradise for Your Friends

I had the honor of knowing a "true beauty," a real princess. Her name was Rachel. On her campus at school, she was a cheerleader and class president with lots of hope for the future. But at the young age of thirteen, Rachel was diagnosed with cancer and given only three to six months to live. I called Rachel as soon as I heard the sad news, and she said, "Sheri Rose, please pray that I can tell all my friends about Jesus before I die so I can see them all again."

I was so touched by Rachel's beautiful heart. Although she was dying and her dreams on earth were ending, she cared more about giving her friends directions to where she was going. Rachel lived until she was sixteen. On her sixteenth birthday, she announced, "I'm ready to go to heaven now. I finished my purpose here on earth." A few weeks later Rachael died. As she took her last breath, she smiled a big smile and said, "Jesus."

She wrote a very special letter to her friends before she died. It read:

> *Dear friend, do not be sad for me today, because I am in Paradise where there is no more sickness and no more death, celebrating my eternal new life. My only wish is that I will get to see you someday on the other*

side of eternity. Jesus is your way to cross over. So please pray to receive Him as your Savior before it's too late, and you check into the wrong place forever without God.

Over a hundred kids from Rachel's school prayed the "Passport Prayer" to Paradise and received the Crown of Life at her funeral. Rachel's beauty will be marked in her friends forever.

Film Your Faith

What about you? If you were to die tomorrow, what would people remember you for? Would they say you touched their lives? Would your parents remember how much you loved on them? What do you want people to remember you for? I know I'm going deep right now, but your life was given to you for a divine purpose. God placed a gift inside of you. It's time to open it and give it away. Don't waste what time you have left here. Start playing your part today in the movie of life. Leave pictures of your actions and choices for people to model after you're gone.

Maybe you already have your passport as you are reading this book, but you haven't been willing to give directions to your friends who love you. My best friend, Karen, watched me go through my parents' divorce, my drug problems, my boy issues and my eating disorder and never once offered to pray me though my pain or invite me to church. She said that she was afraid to talk to me about God. If only she would not have been ashamed of God and His life-changing words in the Bible!

If you are reading this book right now, and you are a Christian, you have the passport to Paradise. Don't be scared or embarrassed to talk about God. People need help finding their way. Look around you. Very few people will reject prayer. I'm not saying you have to start a student crusade on campus, but I want you to offer to pray for them when they need help and invite them to church.

> **" Right now is the time to give all you have, good or bad, to the only One who can help you. "**

Some of you have been hurt so badly by someone that you feel your life is worthless. If you are in pain, no matter what someone did to hurt you, I promise that God can turn it around for good. Pray for your Passport. Let God give you a new life. Forgive and let go of the pain. Right now is the time to give all you have, good or bad, to the only One who can help you. I know that healing takes time. But the clock won't start until God sets it for you. Not only will He set it, but He will also restore the time you lost.

Let me walk you through the Passport Prayer to heaven. It would be my privilege to pray with you now.

❀ Passport PRAYER to Paradise ❀

> Dear God, thank You for sending Your Son, Jesus, as my passport. I ask You now to place that passport in my heart. Forgive me for living life my way. I want to receive my new life here on earth. Amen.

There is something so soothing to your soul when you surrender to God. It's the Holy Spirit, whom God gives to every Christian. Do you realize that at the very moment you prayed, real angels were singing and celebrating in heaven for you? And now you and I will get to meet personally someday. How exciting!

Until we meet in heaven, remember what we've talked about together. I could not have written the words of wisdom in this book if I had not read them from the best-selling book of all times, the Bible. I call it my **B**asic **I**nstructions **B**efore **L**eaving **E**arth. Read about your new life every day, and watch what God does in you and for you.

God Is the Producer and Director of Life

God's character acted out through you is the real "Oscar Trophy" worth winning, because it's a powerful performance that changes people's lives. So keep practicing your talent with your heart, and memorize your lines in the Script (the Bible). If you take your role in God's movie of life seriously, you will be the spotlight in someone's darkness. You will be the star that points to heaven. You will be the director who instructs a lost soul back to God, and you'll be the audience for someone who needs to be applauded for their performance.

Don't wait for the right part to come to you. Play your part every day so that when the Producer calls you will be ready.

Dear God, help me to cast all my cares and insecurities on You so You can cast me in Your movie of life. Let me be the character You created me to be.

GOD TALKS
Eternity

God Is... the CEO/President of Paradise

As you finish this book, God is preparing a place for you. He is the only thing that will matter when we are done with this life. Don't lose your eternal perspective. Keep your passport close to your heart as a reminder that you are not home yet. You are just visiting this place for the purpose of helping people find their eternal destination. You are not responsible for other's actions or reactions to God's great message, but you are responsible for your own actions.

Remember that you can't change anyone but yourself. But your life can change the way people see the "President of Paradise."

It was a drug dealer's changed life that pointed me to God. Live the royal life; put on your crown and banner, which says, "I am a daughter of the King."

I look forward to celebrating with you one day on the other side of eternity.

Dear God, thank You for giving me my passport to Paradise.

May he give you the desire of your heart and make all your plans succeed. We will shout for joy when you are victorious and will lift up our banners in the name of our God.

—PSALM 20:4–5

Notes

Chapter 2: Talent Talk

1. Florence Littauer, *Personality Plus* (Grand Rapds, MI: Fleming H. Revell Co., 1992).

Chapter 3: Girlfriend Talk

1. Source obtained from the Internet: www.teenpregnancy.org/resources/data/genlfact.asp.
2. Source obtained from the Internet: www.alcohol-drug-abuse.com/statistics.htm.
3. Source obtained from the Internet: www.aegis.org/news/ads/1996/ad960421.html.
4. Source obtained from the Internet: www.aegis.org/news/ads/1991/ad910611.html.
5. Source obtained from the Internet: www.stv.net/us_stats.htm.
6. Ibid.
7. Source obtained fro the 1999 National Youth Gang Survey at http://www.ncjrs.org/txtfiles1/ojjdp/fs200020.txt.
8. Ibid.

Chapter 6: Heart-to-Heart Talk

1. William Dufty, *Sugar Blues* (New York: Warner Books, 1993).

More Fun, Food, and Freedom with Sheri Rose Shepherd

"Sheri Rose's pithy offerings are full of playfulness and poignancy - prepare to giggle and grow!"

~**Patsy Clairmont,** author, humorist, Woman of Faith speaker

1-57673-747-0, *Multnomah Publishers*

"Sheri Rose Shepherd proves that eating well does not have to mean deprivation. Delicious recipes and sound advice will make you feel satisfied, self-assured, and energized."

—Fit Magazine editor-in-chief

Join former food addict Sheri Rose Shepherd and enjoy *Eating for Excellence.* You'll discover what foods to eat for your body type, life-safety rules, fat-busters, and the energy-boosting recipes that helped Sheri Rose take off—and keep off—more than 60 pounds.

1-57673-487-0, *Multnomah Publishers*

Sheri Rose at age 16, and today.

If someone you love is battling a food addiction or an eating disorder, make sure you get a copy of the national bestseller, *Fit for Excellence,* and discover God's design for freedom.

8054-6355-0-8, *Creation House Publishers*

More Life-Changing Materials from Sheri Rose Shepherd

In the **7 Ways to Build a Better You** video series, Sheri Rose uses humor, heartwarming stories, and God's Word to teach emotional, physical, relational, and spiritual excellence. In just seven weekly sessions, you'll discover how to get out of the mindset of mediocrity and enter into the spirit of excellence. The 7 Ways series is fun, motivating, inspiring, and easy to apply to everyday life.

Video Series
7-Session, 4-Tape
ISBN 1-57673-607-5
(Includes 64-page workbook)!

Audio Series
7-Session, 4-Tape
ISBN 1-57673-603-2
(Includes 64-page workbook)!

facilitator's guide
ISBN 1-57673-604-0

study guide
ISBN 1-57673-606-7

For product information, call 888-777-2439
P.O. Box 3500 Suite 227 Sisters, OR 97759 www.girltalkministries.com

It's Time...
to Become the
Best Version of YOU!

Schedule Sheri Rose Shepherd to speak
at a conference or retreat in your area.

Hope, Humor, and Hot Topics! Including:

- Barbie Bondage...Mind Over Media

- Lose Weight without Losing Your Mind

- Becoming the Best Version of You

- Energize Your Life

- Break Through to the Blesssed Life

- God in Action

FREE audio tape for
all minstry leaders!

We know you have enjoyed *GirlTalk*, and now it's time to explore other resources for young women!

If you have a heart for the purpose and destiny of girls, you'll get excited as you discover the following products from Strang Communications:

Fit for Excellence!
by Sheri Rose Shepherd

"I encourage women's ministry leaders and pastors to incorporate this teaching into their ministries. This book is a wonderful program to offer in Sunday school classes, women's groups and outreach programs."
—Randy Carlson, Host of *Parent Talk* and president, Family Life Communications

Spirit Led Woman
For the woman who is hungry to know God intimately!

Spiritled Woman is a bimonthly publication that calls women of all ages to step into their destiny by the power of the Holy Spirit. Each issue challenges, instructs and encourages women to step out in faith and passionately pursue God in every area of their lives.

GIRL TALK
Doodle page

GIRL TALK
Doodle page

GIRL TALK
Doodle page

GIRL TALK
Doodle page

GIRL TALK
Doodle page